DEAD BALL

MAJOR LEAGUE
BASEBALL BEFORE
BABE RUTH

THOMAS GILBERT

DEAD BALL

MAJOR LEAGUE

BASEBALL BEFORE

BABE RUTH

THOMAS GILBERT

THE AMERICAN GAME

FRANKLIN WATTS
A Division of Grolier Publishing
New York / London / Hong Kong / Sydney
Danbury, Connecticut

Cover photographs copyright ©: Transcendental Graphics: black and white on left and color inset; National Baseball Library & Archive, Cooperstown, NY: black and white on right.

Photographs copyright ©: Transcendental Graphics: pp. 8, 16, 22, 31, 45, 90, 93, 95, 107, 142, 158; National Baseball Library & Archive, Cooperstown, NY: pp. 40, 41, 61, 62, 69, 77, 103, 113, 115, 130, 152; AP/Wide World Photos: p. 122.

Library of Congress Cataloguing-in-Publication Data

Gilbert, Thomas W.
Dead ball : major-league baseball before Babe Ruth / Thomas Gilbert.
p. cm. — (The American game)
Includes bibliographical references (p.) and index.
Summary: Gives the history of major-league baseball from the late nineteenth to the early twentieth century.
ISBN 0-531-11262-4
1. Baseball—United States—History—19th century—Juvenile literature.
2. Baseball—United States—History—20th century—Juvenile literature.
[1. Baseball—History.] I. Title. II. Series: Gilbert, Thomas W. American game.
GV863.A1G574 1996
796.357′0973′09041—dc20
96-5120
CIP
AC

CONTENTS

CHAPTER ONE
"Clean, Honorable Play":
Monopoly War IV and the Birth of the American League
7

CHAPTER TWO
Small Ball:
Baseball without the Home Run
32

CHAPTER THREE
Big Six, the Cyclone, and the Big Train:
A Generation of Pitching Heroes
55

CHAPTER FOUR
Touching Second:
The Merkle Blunder and the Greatest Pennant Races Ever
73

CHAPTER FIVE
Against the Grain:
Honus Wagner and Ty Cobb
86

CHAPTER SIX
"It's Great to Be Young and a Giant!":
Dead-ball Dynasties
100

CHAPTER SEVEN
Palaces of the Fans:
The First Ballparks Built to Last
126

CHAPTER EIGHT
Tip-Tops and Terrapins:
Monopoly War V and the Federal League
134

CHAPTER NINE
A Corkscrew Mind:
Hal Chase and the Corruption of Major-league Baseball
147

Source Notes
162

Bibliography
164

Appendix A:
Major Leagues, Teams, and Cities (1871–1957)
166

Appendix B:
Index of Major-league Cities and Team Names (1871–1957)
169

Index
173

CHAPTER ONE

"Clean, Honorable Play": Monopoly War IV and the Birth of the American League

Baseball began in New York City in the 1840s as a casual pastime played by no more than a few dozen Wall Street clerks and shopkeepers. Only 20 years later, however, baseball had spread across the United States and was known as America's national game. In 1871 the National Association, the first professional league, was formed. National Association clubs sold tickets and paid their players salaries. Baseball was no longer a simple pastime; it had become a business. In 1876 this league went under and was replaced by the National League—the same National League that is still doing business today.

Under its founder and leader, a wholesale grocer from Chicago named William Hulbert, the National League pioneered the idea of professional baseball as an economic monopoly. Hulbert and his fellow NL magnates achieved dominance over other professional leagues and reduced them to minor-league status; got control of the players by establishing the reserve clause, which bound players to one club indefinitely; and

DEAD BALL!

This cartoon depicts the plight of the batter in the dead-ball era. From 1900–1919, major-league pitchers dominated hitters.

tightly controlled the number, ownership, and location of major-league franchises. If you were a wealthy would-be baseball investor in the 1870s, 1880s, or 1890s, no matter how much money or how big a potential baseball market you had, the only way you could become a member of the National League monopoly was if the other owners let you in. This exclusivity increased the power of the major-league owners, but it created a great deal of tension as fans, cities, and potential owners who were shut out of the major-league monopoly clamored to get a piece of the action.

Throughout the last quarter of the 19th century, a pattern was repeated in which this tension would lead those on the outside to form their own major league and launch an attack on the NL's monopoly; a war would then follow—over markets, over the loyalty of the fans and the press, and, most of all, over the control of player contracts. In the end, the NL won each of these wars: Monopoly War I against the American Association (after losing many of the early battles), Monopoly War II against the Union Association, and Monopoly War III against the Players League. When the year 1900 came along, the National League had outlasted four other major leagues and stood alone atop a vast structure of lesser minor leagues, from which it could take its choice of the best players.

In spite of this unbroken string of victories, however, the National League seemed far from invulnerable as the new century dawned. Many felt that the major-league monopoly had never been weaker. There was even talk of reviving the moribund American Association, which had existed as a major league alongside the NL from 1882 to 1891. Rumor had it that disaffected baseball heavyweights—such as former Chicago White Stockings star Adrian "Cap" Anson, Baltimore Orioles manager John McGraw, prominent sports editor Alfred Spink, former St. Louis Browns owner Chris Von der Ahe, and respected baseball writer Francis Richter of Philadelphia—were involved. Another group that welcomed the idea of a second major league was the newly formed Players' Protective Organization, the latest of many attempts by the players at forming a union that would stand up for their rights. Thanks to the reserve clause, for most of the late 19th century major-league players were trapped in serflike servitude to their employers, with little ability to negotiate fair salaries and no say at all about where they played or for whom. Only during the brief periods of competition for players' services between the NL and a rival major league were the players able to raise salaries or gain a small portion of the rights that players enjoy today. Ten years earlier, the players had united under John Montgomery Ward, rejected the reserve clause, and actually seceded from the major-league monopoly. They set up their own player-run league, called the Players League, that lasted one year before being sold out by its financial backers for a piece of the major-league pie. Since then, the players had endured the return of the reserve clause, reduced rosters, and both team and individual salary limits. As a result, player salaries declined steadily throughout the dreary 1890s.

What was wrong with the National League in 1900? One problem was that the league had operated through most of the 1890s with 12 teams playing in a single-division format. This meant that in a given year at least seven or eight teams were out of the pennant race almost from the beginning; it was virtually impossible to climb over six or seven teams in a 130- or 140-game pennant race. Fans of teams that were 20 or 30 games out of the running naturally lost interest and stopped buying tickets. It also meant that there was no post-season World Series. Back in the American Association (AA) days in the 1880s, baseball fans had enjoyed annual postseason showdowns between the NL and AA pennant winners; the best the NL of the 1890s could do was the Temple Cup Series, which matched the pennant winner against the club that finished second. The Temple Cup Series never caught on and was retired for lack of interest in 1897.

Adding to the problems of the 12-team NL was the fact that the same teams seemed to win the pennant every year. In his 1977 autobiography, *Baseball As I Have Known It,* sportswriter Fred Lieb recalled the frustration of being a young Phillies fan during the 1890s and looking at the baseball standings to find that "teams whose city name started with a B—Baltimore, Boston, and Brooklyn—were always at the top." This was no exaggeration: Brooklyn won the NL pennant in 1890 and 1899; Boston won in 1891, 1892, 1893, 1897, and 1898; Baltimore won in 1894, 1895, and 1896. Two of these clubs deserve a place on the list of the greatest dynasties of all time: the slick Boston Beaneaters—believe it or not, that is what they were called; the team symbol was a pot of baked beans—of Frank Selee, Billy Nash, Hugh Duffy, Tommy McCarthy, Mike "King" Kelly, and Jimmy Collins; and the super-aggressive Baltimore Orioles of Ned Hanlon, "Wee Willie" Keeler, John McGraw, Hughie Jennings, Joe Kelley, and Wilbert Robinson. Both of these clubs were offensive power-houses, pioneering new tactics, such as the hit-and-run and bunt-and-run, and perfecting old tactics like the bunt and the stolen base in order to break down opposing defenses. The Orioles broke down their share of umpires as well, with a nonstop barrage of verbal and even physical abuse. Umpires of the 1890s frequently fell victim to "accidental" spikings or outright assaults by Hanlon, McGraw, and others.

Although the fans of Boston and Baltimore gloried in their clubs' high-scoring, hard-running, psychologically intimidating brand of baseball, many in and out of baseball felt that their rowdy, even dirty, style of play had given the NL a bad name and driven away middle-class fans. One thing that there was no disagreement on, however, was that major-league baseball as a whole was slowly slipping into an economic coma during the 1890s. In 1891, the last year of the American Association, the 16 major-league clubs drew a little over 2,600,000 fans, or an average of more than 164,000 per team; the following year the 12-team NL drew only 1,332,730 fans, or an average of less than 152,000 per team. In a 150-game season, that means most NL games of the 1890s drew 1,000 to 3,000 people, fewer fans than many college or Single-A minor-league contests draw today and far fewer than today's average major-league crowd of 20,000 or so. Although NL attendance did rise a bit in the early 1890s, it peaked in 1895 and 1896 and then once again began to decline. It did not help that the bad teams of the 1890s were among the worst big-league clubs of all time. In 1897 and 1898 eight NL teams finished more than 20 games out of first place. Some of these clubs make the 1962 Mets, the emblem of modern baseball ineptitude, look like an all-star team. In 1898 last-place St. Louis finished at 39–111, and in 1899 Cleveland went 20–134 to finish an amazing 84 games out.

Poor performances like these and generally poor attendance around the league led the NL to drop four franchises—Baltimore, Louisville, Cleveland, and Washington—and play the 1900 season with only eight teams. Nothing much changed. In many ways, the 1900 season was the final season of baseball 1890s-style. It featured great performances by hard-hitting veteran sluggers like Joe Kelley and Big Ed Delahanty and high-average base thieves like Sliding Billy Hamilton and Wee Willie Keeler—and lots and lots of runs. Four teams batted over .280 and stole over 200 bases; Pittsburgh hit 100 triples. The year 1900 also featured a typically dull pennant race, as five of the eight clubs finished 17 or more games out of first place. "Iron Man" Joe McGinnity won a league-leading 29 games pitching in the old underhand style that would soon be swept into oblivion by the new generation of overhand fireballers led by Denton "Cy" Young, George "Rube" Waddell, and Christy Mathewson. Continuing another theme of the bleak 1890s, human misery, Boston catcher Marty Bergen shocked the baseball world by committing suicide after killing his wife and two children in a fit of insane rage. Finally, Ned Hanlon's

Brooklyn Superbas, yet another "B" team, won the NL pennant.

THE YEAR: 1900

Many people are confused about whether 1900 was the last year of the 19th century or the first year of the 20th. In a baseball sense, the confusion is appropriate, because the 1900 season stood astride two historical eras.

Nineteen hundred was the last of nine seasons in which the National League was the only major league. It was also the first year that the NL abandoned the cumbersome 12-team format of the 1890s in favor of the 8-team structure that would remain a part of baseball tradition for the next 61 years.

The year 1900 was the last hurrah for many 1890s stars as well as the last pennant for Ned Hanlon, rivaled only by Boston's Frank Selee as the greatest manager of the late 19th century. When Hanlon left Baltimore for Brooklyn in 1899, he had brought with him the heart of the old Orioles dynasty: two-time batting champion and .400-hitter Wee Willie Keeler, slugger Joe Kelley, and slick-fielding shortstop and 100-RBI man Hughie Jennings. After going 101–47 and winning the pennant in 1899, Hanlon took advantage of Baltimore and Brooklyn's common ownership to return to the Orioles' well for another infusion of talent. Among Hanlon's new prizes were Joe McGinnity, Frank Kitson, Gene DeMontreville, and Jimmy Sheckard. In 1900 Brooklyn put up the kind of offensive numbers that would soon become endangered species in the coming dead-ball era. Their 816 runs scored were the most by an NL team until 1912, after the livelier cork-centered ball had been introduced.

Hanlon's rebuilt Superbas, as the Dodgers were then known (the nickname was a play on the name of a popular vaudeville troupe, Hanlon's Superbas), won 19 fewer games than the year before but still came in 4½ games ahead of a Pittsburgh team that featured two great stars of the future: shortstop John "Honus" Wagner, who led the league in batting at .381, doubles with 45, and triples with 22; and eccentric strikeout pitcher Rube Waddell, who gave a hint of what was to come by whiffing 130 and winning the ERA title at 2.37. Waddell would go on to lead his league in strikeouts six times and finish with a career ERA of 2.16, the sixth-best in history. McGinnity bettered his 1899 win total of 28 by one game and led the league in innings pitched with 347.

The downsizing of the league to eight teams would come back to haunt the NL magnates, as Cleveland, Washington, Louisville, and Baltimore joined the long list of lucrative baseball markets that the major-league monopoly had abandoned or refused to exploit. Between 1882 and 1890, there had been major-league franchises, at one time or another, in 26 different cities across the East, the Middle Atlantic, the Midwest, and the West. Those cities were Boston, Baltimore, Buffalo, Chicago, Cincinnati, Cleveland, Detroit, Indianapolis, Kansas City, New York, Philadelphia, Pittsburgh, Providence, St. Louis, Troy, Washington, Worcester, Brooklyn, Columbus, Louisville, Richmond, Toledo, Altoona, Milwaukee, St. Paul, and Wilmington. By cutting that number down to eight, the NL cut off whole regions of the country, containing millions of fans, from major-league baseball. Six of the NL cities in 1900 were located in the East, four of them on the East Coast; only Chicago and St. Louis could have been called western cities in 1900. Big cities like Detroit, Washington, Cleveland, Baltimore, and Milwaukee had major-league-caliber fans and major-league-caliber investors. The only thing that stood between them and their rightful place in the major leagues was the greed and shortsightedness of the handful of men who controlled the baseball monopoly. The forces that would bring Monopoly War IV were brewing.

In each previous monopoly war, the NL had been united under a strong, capable leader like William Hulbert or Albert Spalding. The men in charge of baseball in 1900, however, were incapable of agreeing on what to order for lunch, much less on how to wage the coming monopoly war. Monopoly War IV was different from earlier wars in that the NL was distracted, leaderless, and irreconcilably divided into two ownership factions: one led by Albert Spalding and another led by New York Giants owner Andrew Freedman. Spalding was a former star pitcher of the 1870s who retired in his twenties to found the Spalding Sporting Goods company. Now a millionaire, Spalding owned the Chicago NL club. Freedman was a shadowy figure with connections to New York City's unsavory Tammany Hall political machine; he had made a vast fortune in subway construction and insurance, two areas of business where his political muscle came in very handy. After buying the New York Giants in 1895, Freedman had made a nuisance of himself, firing managers at a Steinbrenneresque pace, feuding with players and fellow owners alike, and generally running that glorious franchise into the ground. Always willing to trade ten dollars tomorrow for one dollar today, Freedman was, in many ways, a typical baseball owner of his time. As Albert Spalding explains in his 1911 book, *Baseball: America's National Game,* in the 1890s baseball's biggest problem was not the traditional triad of gambling, fan rowdiness, and player corruption, but rather "club officials, generally termed *magnates,* and it will be readily understood how difficult a matter it was to deal with them. Especially it was hard to reach cases where there was no actual violation of baseball law—just personal cussedness and disregard for the future welfare of the game."[1]

Albert Spalding—sporting goods tycoon, owner of the Chicago NL club, and former star pitcher—made a stand against syndicate baseball in 1901.

Part of what Spalding is talking about here is the phenomenon of common, or overlapping, ownership of two different baseball clubs, or "syndicate baseball" as it was then called. One notorious example was the transfer of Orioles manager Ned Hanlon and many of his best players to Brooklyn by Harry Van der Horst, who owned interests in both teams. Another was the looting of the Cleveland Spiders' roster by owner Frank Robison, who transferred Cy Young, Patsy Tebeau, Clarence "Cupid" Childs, Jesse Burkett, and other top-quality players to his St. Louis club in 1899, making possible the Spiders' infamous 20–134 record and ultimate ejection from the league. Maneuvers such as these served the short-term interests of the owners involved, but they alienated fans and cost the NL an incalculable amount of prestige.

In 1900, Andrew Freedman wanted to extend the idea of syndicate baseball even further by reorganizing the NL into one big syndicate with common ownership. Clubs would no longer be independent competitors, bidding against each other for playing talent, but subsidiaries of a giant corporation. The owners would be business partners; managers and players would be employees of the league, with equivalent players being paid identical salaries, and would be allocated to each team according to the wishes of a central board of directors. The goal was what today's owners call "cost certainty" and an end to bidding wars between clubs for players' services; the owners would be guaranteed a tidy profit whether their teams performed well or not. The only losers would be the players, who would be paid less, and the fans, who would be cheated of any real competition between the clubs. Four clubs supported Freedman's idea, which became known as Freedmanism, and four clubs supported Al Spalding, who vehemently opposed it. For months, these two factions locked horns over Freedmanism—and everything else. When it came time to elect a new NL president in 1901, the vote was four for Spalding and four for Nick Young, Freedman's candidate. The owners struggled in vain for a way to break the tie; 25 ballots later, the vote remained deadlocked at four to four. Finally, Spalding attempted to take office illegally, and Freedman responded by getting an injunction from a New York State court that forbade Spalding from taking office. Spalding evaded the injunction by remaining outside New York. This was the predicament the NL found itself in when the American League fired the first shot in Monopoly War IV by declaring itself a major league on January 28, 1901.

The AL may have picked the best possible time to take on the NL, but the timing of Monopoly War IV was at least partly a matter of luck. The story of the AL began back in 1893, well before the fight over Freedmanism, when Cincinnati player-manager Charles Comiskey and sportswriter Ban Johnson struck up a friendship at a bar called the Ten-Minute Club (so named because customers had to order a round of drinks every 10 minutes or be asked to leave). Both men loved baseball and loved the outdoors. During hunting, fishing, and canoeing trips in the Wisconsin wilderness, Comiskey and Johnson talked about the possibility of someday raising a minor league to major-league status and taking advantage of the many, mostly western, baseball markets that had been shut out of the 12-team NL.

Johnson was an imperious, hard-drinking, cigar-smoking Ohioan. He was the proud descendant of an illustrious Yankee family that had left Connecticut for the Western frontier in the 1840s. Both his father and grandfather were educators, and an uncle, Rossiter Johnson, was a prominent journalist who had edited several famous encyclopedias and history books. A talented catcher in those days before face masks or catcher's equipment of any kind, Ban Johnson played baseball in college well enough to receive a contract offer from a big-league club. Coincidentally, Johnson attended Oberlin College only a class or two ahead of fellow catcher Moses Fleetwood Walker, who would go on to become the major leagues' first African-American player with Toledo of the American Association in 1884. Johnson's father, however, forbade him to enter such a disreputable profession as baseball; presumably the elder Johnson considered sports journalism an acceptable compromise between Ban's love of baseball and the family's good name.

This may have been the last time anybody told Ban Johnson what to do. From his first job as a cub reporter to his ascension to the sports editorship of the influential *Cincinnati Commercial-Gazette,* Johnson displayed a fearless independence combined with an acid pen. He never let anybody or anything move him one millimeter from what he thought was right and seemed to relish making powerful enemies. A favorite editorial theme was "foul [playing] tactics" and the poor public image of baseball. According to biographer Eugene Murdock, "Ban crusaded endlessly against rowdy behavior, a crusade allied to another favorite cause; the dignity and professionalization of the umpire."[2]

Born in Chicago and the son of popular Irish-born politician "Honest" John Comiskey, Charles Comiskey played first base and managed the great St. Louis Browns dynasty that dominated the American Association in the 1880s. He was now winding down his career with the NL Cincinnati Reds. Even though Comiskey got along well with Reds owner John T. Brush, he was restless and longed to trade in his spikes and knickers for the three-piece suit of an executive. Comiskey's opportunity came shortly after a meeting in Detroit on November 20, 1893, where minor-league operators from Grand Rapids, Sioux Falls, Minneapolis, Milwaukee, Kansas City, Toledo, Indianapolis, and Detroit met to revive the Western League (WL), a minor league that had gone belly-up the year before. Comiskey attended the meeting as the representative of Brush, who, as the owner of both the Indianapolis club and the major-league Reds, was the most powerful of the WL backers. When the time came to elect a president, secretary, and treasurer for the new league, Comiskey painted such a glowing portrait of his friend Ban Johnson that the WL clubs elected him to fill all three offices.

A year later, Ban Johnson's success was the talk of minor-league baseball. He had built up a corps of competent umpires and made good on his vow to back them all the way against attacks by players or managers—an umpire's life in some minor leagues could be even rougher than in the big leagues; a few minor-league umpires actually carried guns while on duty—improved security at the sometimes disorderly WL ballparks, and put the league on a solid financial footing. Attendance and profits were up, and fewer and fewer franchises went broke or found it necessary to move to another city after the season. When John T. Brush, jealous of Johnson's success and independence—and remembering some of the unflattering columns Johnson had written about him in the *Commercial-Gazette*—tried to have him defeated for reelection as WL president, Comiskey took Johnson's side. He resigned as manager of the Reds, borrowed a few thousand dollars, and bought the St. Paul WL club (which had moved from Sioux Falls). First baseman Charles Comiskey was now an executive.

The next few years gave Johnson and Comiskey valuable lessons in the baseball business and in the many ways the National League took advantage of the

WL and other minor leagues. At that time, most minor-league clubs were independently owned and not subsidiaries, or farm teams, of major-league organizations, as they are today. In order to protect their rosters and markets from raiding by the NL, however, a majority of the minor leagues had signed onto the National Agreement, which gave minor-league clubs some protections but also gave major-league clubs the right to draft minor-league players for a fixed draft price. The WL's biggest problem was that Brush, as owner of both WL Indianapolis and NL Cincinnati, could move players back and forth between the two clubs as needed. This meant that if Indianapolis were scheduled to face, say, Comiskey's St. Paul club in a game that might decide the WL pennant, Indianapolis could borrow a major-league pitcher from Cincinnati for that one game. It also meant that Brush could draft a top player from any rival WL club onto the Reds' roster and then send him down to the Indianapolis club. Despite repeated protests from Johnson and other minor-league executives, the NL adamantly refused to raise the draft price from $500 to a more reasonable $1,000.

The NL refused to modify the National Agreement to deal with any of the problems caused by dual minor-league/major-league ownership. Thanks to the unfair advantage that this gave Brush, Indianapolis won the WL pennant in 1895, 1897, and 1899 and finished second in 1896 and 1898. Nevertheless the league as a whole was stronger than ever going into the 1900 season: Fans in WL cities continued to respond to Johnson's clean, disciplined brand of baseball; most clubs were making money; and, as Johnson himself said proudly, "[a WL] umpire was no longer a bad [life] insurance risk." Besides Comiskey, Johnson's strong leadership had attracted into the WL talented, energetic baseball men like former Pittsburgh catcher Cornelius

21

UMPIRING MADE EASY.

A Hint for the New York Nine.—Give the Umpire a Chance.

A cartoon from Puck *magazine shows the hazards of umpiring at the turn of the century.*

McGillicuddy, whose name had to be amputated to Connie Mack so that it would fit into a newspaper box score, and Milwaukee owner Matt Killilea.

During the off-season of 1899–1900, the WL changed its name to the grander American League (AL), a clear indication of its major-league ambitions. The NL owners did not get the hint. Shortly afterward, distracted by the rumored rebirth of the American Association, the NL made its first blunder in dealing with

Johnson and Comiskey's league. The NL allowed Comiskey to move his St. Paul club into Chicago under the venerable name White Stockings, or, as it soon appeared in the newspapers, the White Sox. This was a name that the NL Cubs had used for much of the 19th century. Cubs owner Jim Hart, the executive who had somewhat heavy-handedly forced the legendary Cap Anson into retirement, agreed to the move on two conditions: first, that Comiskey's team play on the working-class South Side, close to the foul-smelling stockyards and slaughterhouses and far away from the NL Cubs' tonier West Side Park; and second, that it would not call itself the *Chicago* White Sox. Now consisting of clubs playing near-major-league caliber baseball in major cities like Chicago, Indianapolis, Buffalo, Detroit, Cleveland, Milwaukee, Minneapolis, and Kansas City, the AL of 1900 was poised in a kind of limbo between minor-league and major-league status.

At the end of the 1900 season, the agreement that bound the old Western League to the National Agreement expired, and Johnson made no effort to renew it. It seemed obvious to everyone but the men in charge of the National League that the AL was about to proclaim itself a major league. Ban Johnson hoped that the NL would be reasonable and negotiate some kind of co-major-league status for the AL, but he was preparing for the worst. Johnson developed a secret strategy that involved moving AL franchises into NL strongholds Boston and Philadelphia for the 1901 season, raiding NL reserve lists for unsigned players, and declaring all-out economic war. As in Chicago, the new AL clubs would adopt nostalgic team nicknames that had been discarded by the older NL franchises; the Boston club would call itself the Red Stockings, or Red Sox, after Harry Wright's powerhouse of the 1870s, and the Philadelphia club would revive the name Athletics, which dated back to baseball's pre–Civil War amateur days. During the NL owners' off-season meeting in New York, Johnson sent a telegram from Philadelphia offering to come to New York and discuss a new relationship between the leagues. "They sent back word," Johnson later recalled, "that I could stay there until hell froze over."

Sensing the weakness and division of the older league, deep-pocketed investors like coal millionaire Charles Somers and real estate tycoon John Kilfoyl saw the looming monopoly war as their opportunity to get into the major-league club. Somers and Kilfoyl committed millions of dollars to bankroll the AL invasion of the East; this was on top of huge sums that Somers had already put into the existing Chicago and Cleveland franchises. Men like Somers and Kilfoyl were needed in order to buy land and build ballparks from scratch in several cities and to pay for the large contracts that Johnson's league intended to dangle in front of as many NL stars as possible.

Thanks to more NL blundering, this did not require as much money as Johnson had expected. At the same off-season meeting at which the NL owners snubbed Ban Johnson, they also refused to recognize the new players' union, the Players' Protective Organization, and dismissed the union's proposals for a few modest reforms in the standard baseball contract. For many players, that was the end of any loyalty they might have felt toward the older league.

Johnson and Comiskey took immediate advantage. Like so many earlier upstart major leagues in earlier monopoly wars, the AL appealed to the downtrodden players by rejecting the reserve clause and proclaiming itself the champion of reform and player rights. After a meeting with Charles "Chief" Zimmer and Hughie Jennings of the players' organization, Ban Johnson announced, "They wanted to know if we would agree in our contracts not to farm, trade, or sell players without the players' consent. Of course I agreed to this." Commitments like these would go right out the window the moment Monopoly War IV ended and the owners of the two leagues made peace, but in the meantime they influenced many NL players to consider crossing over to the AL. An AL commando team made up of Chicago pitcher Clark Griffith, owner of the new Philadelphia Athletics Connie Mack, John McGraw, and veteran Cleveland outfielder Jimmy McAleer secretly traveled from NL city to NL city and offered fat AL contracts to a list of 46 picked NL stars who were reserved, but not actually under contract, for 1901.

THE YEAR: 1901

The upstart American League opened for business in Milwaukee, Cleveland, Washington, Baltimore, Detroit, Philadelphia, Boston, and Chicago, the latter three franchises located on prime National League turf. Refusing to respect the NL's reserve clause, Ban Johnson and the AL owners ruthlessly raided NL rosters. Dozens of players—among them big names like Cy Young, Hugh Duffy, and Jimmy Collins—gladly jumped at the chance to change leagues. These stars, and others, lent instant legitimacy to the AL; fans came out in droves to see ex-St. Louis Cardinal Cy Young win 33 games for Boston with a 1.62 ERA, and ex-Chicago NL star Clark Griffith go 24–7 for the crosstown White Sox. But the brightest star of all was second baseman Napoleon Lajoie of Connie Mack's Philadelphia Athletics. Lajoie led the AL in nearly every offensive category in 1901. He batted .422 and slugged .635. Thanks to Lajoie, the A's won their attendance war with the Phillies but finished five games behind Boston and nine games back of a speedy Chicago club that stole 280 bases, led the league in runs and ERA, and finished with a record of 83–53.

In the NL, a relatively intact Pittsburgh Pirates team won that city's first pennant in two decades of major-league competition, compiling a 90–49 record on the strength of pitchers like Jack Chesbro, a spitball virtuoso who went 21–10; Deacon Phillippe, who went 22–12; and Jesse Tannehill, who won the ERA title at 2.18. Pacing the Pirates attack was the outfield duo of Clarence "Ginger" Beaumont and Fred Clarke, both of whom scored 100 runs and batted over .300, and budding superstar Honus Wagner. Wagner stole a league-high 49 bases, batted .353, and drove in 126 runs. Brooklyn's Jimmy Sheckard slugged .536 to lead the league and banged out 19 triples and 11 homers. In New York, a 20-year-old rookie named Christy Mathewson went 20–17 with a 2.41 ERA, the first of his thirteen 20-win seasons. Another future star, Wahoo Sam Crawford, played his first full season in 1901 and hit .330 with a league-leading 16 home runs. Eighteen-nineties legend and two-time .400-hitter Jesse Burkett won his final batting title at .382 for fourth-place St. Louis.

The AL's campaign to attract NL talent succeeded beyond all expectation. The list of former NL greats who played for the AL in 1901 includes Roger Bresnahan, Steve Brodie, Lou Criger, Lave Cross, Jimmy Collins, Harry Davis, Turkey Mike Donlin, Hugh Duffy, John "Jiggs" Donohue, Norman "Kid" Elberfeld, William "Dummy" Hoy, Frank Isbell, Fielder Jones, Joe McGinnity, Sam Mertes, Fred Parent, Wilbert Robinson, Ossee Schreck, James "Cy" Seymour, Cy Young, Charles "Chick" Stahl—and many, many more. By historian Lee Allen's count, 111 out of 182 AL playing jobs in 1901 were held by former National Leaguers.

The player with the biggest impact by far on the baseball balance of power was a 26-year-old Rhode Islander, the son of Quebecois immigrants, named Napoleon "Larry" Lajoie (generally pronounced "Lah'-zhuh-way"). The second baseman batted .328, .363, .328, .380, and .346—good, but certainly not awesome numbers for the high-scoring 1890s—in his first five major-league seasons with the Philadelphia Phillies. In 1901, however, Lajoie jumped to the level of superstar. Playing for the newborn Philadelphia Athletics of the AL, Lajoie put on a one-man slugging exhibition, hitting .422 with 14 home runs and 125 RBIs.

All of these were league-leading figures; had there been such a thing as the Triple Crown Award in 1901, Lajoie would have been the AL's first winner. He led the league in almost everything else, too. He banged out 229 hits in 131 games, scored 145 runs, and stole 27 bases. Lajoie did not lead the AL in triples, the real power statistic of the dead-ball era, but he was among the league leaders with 14. Only one other man, Rogers Hornsby, playing in the home run–happy 1920s, ever led in all three Triple Crown stats with a batting average over .400. Although some discount Lajoie's great numbers, arguing that the AL of 1901 was still a cut below the competitive level of the 1890s NL and pointing out that foul balls were not counted as strikes in the AL in 1901, it must be remembered that all of this was just as true for the men Lajoie outperformed as for Lajoie himself. AL batting title runner-up John "Buck" Freeman of Boston, for example, trailed Lajoie by 77 points at .345; Lajoie scored 25 more runs than the nearest batter and drove in 11 more.

Even Lajoie's heroics could not bring the Athletics the pennant; the team's pitching faltered and they finished fourth. But thousands of Phillies fans followed Lajoie over to the new league, guaranteeing an AL foothold in one of the three key markets (the other two being Chicago and Boston) where Ban Johnson had chosen to fight the NL on its own ground. The young superstar was so important to the AL that his contract status became one of the key battlegrounds of Monopoly War IV. The NL Phillies went to court and obtained an injunction forbidding Lajoie from playing for any Pennsylvania team other than the Phillies for the 1902 season. Knowing how important Lajoie's drawing power was for the survival of the AL, Athletics manager Connie Mack transferred Lajoie to Charles Somers's Cleveland club, where he would be safely outside the Pennsylvania court's jurisdiction. There, with the exception of Cleveland's road games in Philadelphia, Lajoie played out the 1902 campaign, hitting .368.

Lajoie remained with Cleveland for 12 more years, winning two batting titles and seeing the team nicknamed the Naps in his honor. Unlike many sluggers, Lajoie was a complete player; even though he was so muscular that he had to turn down repeated offers to exhibit his chiseled physique in various dime museums and amusement shows, he was agile enough to play a superb second base. As sportswriter Arthur Daley wrote, "[Lajoie] glided with Gallic grace and efficient ease over tremendous stretches of ground. Never did he make a play seem hard. . . . He was the most graceful ballplayer who ever lived." When the Baseball Hall of Fame opened in 1939, Lajoie was the sixth man chosen for induction.

THE YEAR: 1902

Spurred by its success in Chicago, Philadelphia, and Boston, the AL moved its Milwaukee franchise into another NL market, St. Louis. The new team promptly raided the St. Louis Cardinals roster for most of its stars, including Jesse Burkett, Bobby Wallace, and Jack Powell. A further telling blow to the NL was the defection of slugger Big Ed Delahanty from NL Philadelphia to the AL Washington Senators, where he won the AL batting title at .376 and led in doubles with 43 and in slugging average at .590.

In the AL pennant race, Lajoie-less but still hard-hitting Philadelphia won with an 83–53 record, mainly on the strength of Lave Cross's 108 RBIs; Tully "Topsy" Hartsel's league-leading 47 stolen bases, 87 walks, and 109 runs scored; and Ralph "Socks" Seybold's 16 home runs. Seybold set an AL single-season record that lasted until 1919, when a pitcher and part-time outfielder named George "Babe" Ruth swatted the unimaginable total of 29 home runs.

In the NL, Pittsburgh repeated and won a league-record 103 games against 36 losses. The Pirates made a clean sweep of virtually every major offensive and defensive category. Ginger Beaumont won the batting title at .357; Jack Chesbro led in wins with 28 and winning percentage at .824; and Honus Wagner led in runs with 105, RBIs with 91, doubles with 33, stolen bases with 42, and slugging average at .467; Tommy Leach slugged a league-high 23 triples and six homers. Chicago's Jack Taylor turned in a league-best 1.33 ERA, and in a historic iron-man season, Boston's Vic Willis started 46 games (the sixth-most in the 20th century), completed 45 (second-most in the 20th century), and threw 410 innings (the fifth-highest total in 20th-century major-league history).

The war between the leagues continued to be fought hard during the 1902 season. With Lajoie safely out of reach of the NL in Cleveland, the main battle of 1902 was waged in Baltimore. John McGraw's AL career ended almost before it started, as the old NL firebrand and champion umpire-baiter clashed repeatedly with AL president Ban Johnson over McGraw's behavior on the field. In 1901 Johnson had infuriated McGraw by suspending him for verbally abusing an umpire; by early 1902 McGraw was beginning to feel like a marked man. In April, McGraw was treated with a little of his own medicine by umpire Jack Sheridan, who watched stone-faced as Boston's hard-throwing Big Bill Dineen hit McGraw five times with pitches. Each time Sheridan refused to award McGraw first base on the grounds that he had let the ball hit him intentionally. Finally Sheridan added insult to injury by ejecting McGraw from the game. When the Orioles manager appealed to the league, Johnson backed his umpire and suspended McGraw for an additional five days.

McGraw tried to get even with Johnson later in the season when he secretly enlisted two NL owners to buy a controlling interest in the Orioles' stock and then release virtually the entire lineup—including stars Joe Kelley, Roger Bresnahan, and Joe McGinnity—to the New York Giants and the Cincinnati Reds. Shortly afterward, McGraw quit the AL and was hired as manager of the NL Giants. An irate Johnson seized control of the Baltimore franchise and immediately made plans to move it, under pitcher-manager Clark Griffith, into New York to compete with McGraw's Giants.

Despite the loss of McGraw, it became clearer and clearer as 1902 went on that Ban Johnson's new league had won Monopoly War IV. By season's end, the AL had drawn a total of 2,206,454 fans, or over a half million more than the NL's 1,683,012. The NL's attendance leader, New York, was outdrawn by three AL clubs. Significantly, these three clubs—Chicago, Philadelphia, and Boston—were the vanguard of Johnson's strategy of invading prime NL turf. A delegation of NL owners contacted Ban Johnson to cry "uncle," and a peace agreement was negotiated on Johnson's terms. Both eight-team major leagues agreed to respect each other's contracts, reserve lists, and territories, and baseball would be governed by a national commission. This is the two-league, eight-team major-league structure that

30

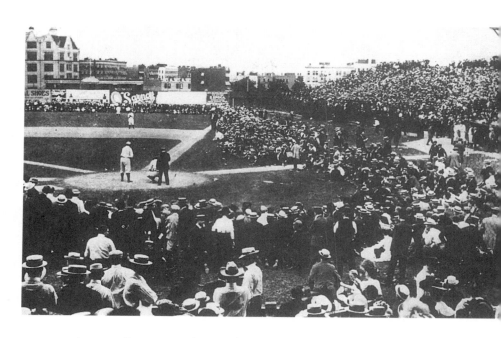

An overflow crowd gets close to the action during a Highlanders-A's game at Hilltop Park, home of the AL New York club.

stood virtually unchanged, without so much as a single franchise shift or expansion, until 1953.

As part of the agreement, incidentally, Griffith and the AL Baltimore Orioles were allowed to move into New York City in 1903. Known at first as the Highlanders, this franchise not only prospered but became the greatest baseball dynasty of all time—the storied New York Yankees of Babe Ruth, Lou Gehrig, Joe DiMaggio, Mickey Mantle, Yogi Berra, and Whitey Ford—and so dominated the New York baseball scene that McGraw's Giants would ultimately be forced to leave town and move 3,000 miles away to San Francisco.

CHAPTER
TWO

*S*mall Ball: Baseball without the Home Run

The National Agreement signed by both major leagues in 1903 set up a three-man National Commission of NL president Harry Pulliam, AL president Ban Johnson, and Cincinnati Reds owner Garry Herrmann. In practice, however, baseball in the dead-ball era was governed by one man: Ban Johnson. Herrmann was an Ohio businessman and politician who had bought the Reds from Johnson's old enemy John Brush—with Andrew Freedman out of baseball, Brush had taken over the NL New York Giants. Herrmann was also a childhood playmate of Johnson's and voted with his old friend on nearly every important matter facing the commission.

During the early 1900s, the National Commission adopted Johnson's entire "clean play" program of respect for umpires, tight control of fan behavior, and marketing the game once again to the respectable middle classes. The program worked. The NL soon lost its rowdy reputation, along with much of its urban, Irish-American flavor; the AL brought a new influx of phlegmatic western and midwestern players. Thanks to baseball's new respectability and the return of the exciting eight-team, two-league format that had thrilled the country's fans back in the 1880s, major-league attendance and club profits began to rise.

Possibly the greatest and most lasting change of the early 1900s, however, was a little-noticed rules change passed by the NL in 1901 and the AL in 1903: the foul-strike rule. Under this rule, foul balls were, for the first time, counted as strikes until there were two strikes on a batter. Previously, during the run-happy 1890s and before, foul balls had not counted at all. The foul-strike rule was intended to quicken the game, as well as to aid major-league pitchers, who had been battered around for years by .400-hitting sluggers like Sam Thompson, Hugh Duffy, Jesse Burkett, and Ed Delahanty to the point that whole teams regularly batted in the .300s. In 1894, the offensive high-water mark of the 1890s, five clubs scored more than 1,000 runs and only two recorded team ERAs under 5.00. As has been the case with so many other attempts to adjust the balance between pitching and hitting in baseball history, this one had consequences that went far beyond what its authors had intended. The foul-strike rule devastated hitting and put pitchers firmly in control of the game for two decades. AL total run scoring fell from 5,407 runs in 1902 to 4,543 in 1903; the league ERA dropped from 3.57 to 2.95, and the number of shutouts nearly doubled. By 1904 it was no longer unusual for a top starting pitcher to record an ERA well under 2.00; the Highlanders' Jack Chesbro completed 325 innings with an ERA of 1.82 and finished fifth in the running for the ERA title in the AL. Not only did run and extra-base hit totals fall, but so did singles, stolen bases, and virtually every other offensive statistic.

In 1904, NL star Honus Wagner of the Pittsburgh Pirates protested publicly that the foul-strike rule was unfair to hitters. Even "scientific baseball" advocate

Henry Chadwick, who had spent a lifetime promoting pitching and defense in favor of the slugging, high-scoring style of baseball, complained. Pitchers dominated the game so completely that the stolen base, bunt, and hit-and-run became hallmarks of what is now termed "small ball" instead of tactics of aggression. As historian Bill James wrote, "With runs becoming dear and outs comparatively cheap, one-run strategies dominated. With a runner on first and nobody out, a bunt was so automatic that most managers didn't even have a sign for it. The hit-and-run, popularized in the previous decade as an aggressive, big-inning tactic, now became a defensive, get-one-base-if-nothing-else maneuver."[1]

The major leagues tried to correct their mistake in 1911 by introducing the cork-centered baseball, but even a livelier ball did not restore batting to anywhere near 1890s levels. Offensive numbers blipped upward only briefly, before falling back to the levels of the 1900s. More than anything else, the foul-strike rule shaped the character of the two pitching-dominated decades that have come to be known as the dead-ball era. In almost every baseball era before or since, the game's greatest stars had been hitters for average and sluggers like Cap Anson, Babe Ruth, Joe DiMaggio, Mickey Mantle, Ted Williams, Willie Mays, Reggie Jackson, Ken Griffey, Jr., or Barry Bonds. Thanks to the foul strike, however, the greatest stars of the first two decades of this century were a group of men who, in most years, struggled to bat their weight: masterful starting pitchers like Christy Mathewson, Cy Young, and Walter Johnson.

THE YEAR: 1903

After the disastrous 1902 season, the National League sued for peace. Ban Johnson rejected the NL's offer to form another 12-team league, and the modern two-major-league format was born. Other points of the new National Agreement included AL adoption of the foul-strike rule and NL acceptance of an AL franchise in New York. The agreement also set up a new National Commission consisting of league presidents Pulliam and Johnson and Johnson ally Garry Herrmann. This arrangement guaranteed Ban Johnson's paramount influence; he would remain the de facto lord of baseball until the gambling scandals of the late 1910s brought about the modern sole baseball commissionership.

Johnson gave pitcher-manager Clark Griffith the job of building a successful AL club in New York City. Partially owned by Tammany Hall figure Joseph Gordon, the club was first called the Highlanders, as a play on both the well-known British army regiment Gordon's Highlanders and the team's hastily constructed park at 165th and Broadway, the highest point in Manhattan. This nickname, however, proved to be about as popular among New York City's numerous Irish-American fans as the Union Jack. By 1904, with a collective thumbing of the nose at the idea of a baseball team nickname with British associations, newspapermen were beginning to call the team the Yankee Highlanders, or simply the Yankees.

Both 1903 pennant races were laughers. AL Boston led the league in runs scored and fewest runs allowed behind slugger Buck Freeman, who hit 13 home runs and drove in 104; fan favorite and runs-scored leader Patsy Dougherty; and pitchers like Cy Young (28–9), Long Tom Hughes (20–7), and Big Bill Dineen (21–13). They finished 14½ games up on a Philadelphia team that featured improved pitching thanks to rookie Charles "Chief" Bender, Eddie Plank, and Rube Waddell, but an attack weakened by off-years from Harry Davis and Lafayette "Lave" Cross. Larry Lajoie's one-man show in Cleveland, including a league-high .355

batting average and .533 slugging average, could push his team no higher than third place, 15 games out.

Nineteenth-century great and legendary drinker Ed Delahanty died one night in 1903 when he was put off a train for disorderly behavior and then pursued the train on foot over a bridge upriver from Niagara Falls; he fell in and drowned. Delahanty's lifetime .346 batting average trails only Rogers Hornsby and Pete Browning among right-handed hitters on the all-time list.

In Honus Wagner's first year as the regular short-stop—he had been a utility man, playing first, third, short, and the outfield—Pittsburgh won its third straight NL pennant with a 91–49 record. Called the Flying Dutchman, Wagner won another batting title at .355, and he and teammates Ginger Beaumont, Fred Clarke, and Tommy Leach monopolized the leader board in most other hitting categories. Second-place New York had the NL's top pitching duo in 31–20 Iron Man McGinnity and 30–13 Christy Mathewson, but McGraw's club never got close enough to make a race of it. McGinnity lived up to his nickname by pitching 48 starts, fourth-most in 20th-century history; 44 complete games, third-most; and 434 innings, the third-highest total ever and 68 more than runner-up Mathewson.

Late in the 1903 season, the owners of the two first-place clubs agreed between themselves to play a best-of-nine postseason world championship series. AL Boston came back to win 5-3 after being down 3–1 to the heavily favored Pirates. Ironically, the star of the series was Pittsburgh's Charles "Deacon" Phillippe, a great control pitcher who, owing to injuries to Pirates starters Sam Leever and Ed Doheny, was forced to pitch an incredible five complete games; he went 3–2 with a 2.86 ERA. The recent war between the leagues and the drama of underdog versus dynasty made the series a big success and led to the establishment of the modern annual World Series, which continued uninterrupted from 1905 until the strike-marred 1994 season.

What was dead-ball baseball really like? If we could travel through time and see a baseball game of the early 1900s for ourselves, we might well pick the first game of a pennant-deciding doubleheader that was played by the Yankees and Red Sox on October 10, 1904.

Monday, October 10, 1904, began as a cool and cloudy day; obviously, it was also a work day for most New York baseball fans. But this did not hurt the gate; neither did the fact that the West Side subway tracks did not yet extend all the way uptown to the New York Yankees' ballpark at 165th Street and Broadway. By one o'clock, the starting time for game one of the doubleheader between New York and Boston, more than 28,000 fans—a New York City record—had crammed themselves into little Hilltop Park, capacity 15,000. Uncounted others were turned away.

Box scores and batting averages from 1904 may look reasonably familiar to us today, but if somehow we were to attend a game like this one—and manage to get a ticket—we would find ourselves in an utterly foreign world. The most immediately striking thing about dead-ball baseball would be its small scale. There were no PA systems or video screens, no polyester uniforms or batting gloves, no relief aces or home-run hitters; tickets cost 50 cents and games routinely finished in less than an hour and a half. In many ways the game of 1904 had an informal, sandlot kind of atmosphere.

No one would have called the Yankees' ballpark, a ramshackle wooden affair with a single deck, a stadium. It had been thrown up in a matter of months in 1903 with the expectation that it would last about as long as other facilities of its kind; that is, it would either fall down or burn down within five or ten years. Our first big surprise upon entering the stands, after getting over the shock of having our ticket taken by one of the Yankees' bench players—in uniform!—would be the state of the field: sloping, rocky, and covered only here and there by lonely patches of grass. Right field featured what one newspaper termed a "ravine" surrounded by a low fence for the safety of the outfielders. A ball hit into this area became a ground-rule triple. One reason for the field's disrepair is immediately clear; for big games, the fans overflow onto the outfield to stand behind ropes and even along the foul lines. This necessitates another set of ground rules: a fair ball hit into the fans goes for a triple or, in the case of extraordinary crowds like this one, only two bases.

As for the crowd itself, it bears little resemblance to the age, gender, race, and class cross section that can be encountered at a modern baseball game. Nineteen-hundred-and-four is a time when public social life in America is almost exclusively male, white, and well-to-do; the crowd at this game is a typical one. They are nearly all white men, and their canes, dark suits, and derby hats make the point that they are nearly all white-collar workers. With games normally scheduled for late afternoons after banker's hours, six days a week, a working-class fan is a very rare sight. There are no lights for night games, and the Northeast's traditional blue laws prohibit playing on Sunday. Only a few expensively dressed and bonneted women watch from the field boxes.

Thanks to a group of boisterous Bostonians known as the Royal Rooters, there is one African-American in attendance. He is a 70-year-old man named Gabriel Hazard, who has been hired by the Rooters to act as their mascot; this entails dancing and shuffling atop the visitors' dugout to "Dixie" or "Old Black Joe" as played by Dockstader's minstrel band, a popular blackface act. According to the *Boston Herald,* "[Hazard] carried a bean pot on top of a pole and was marched in front of the grandstand, much to the edification of the crowd, which cheered heartily, while some of the New York players ran their hands through his wool [hair] for luck." No one in a 1904 major-league grandstand would have taken this as anything other than good, clean fun.

Several hundred Royal Rooters, among them the immortal baseball character Mike "Nuf Sed" McGreevy, had come to New York by specially chartered train to serenade the Red Sox with their theme song, "Tessie." McGreevy, whose nickname derived from his status as Boston's unofficial final authority on all baseball matters, ran a saloon by the name of Third Base around the corner from the Red Sox' Huntington Avenue Baseball Grounds; a famous billboard inside the park posed the question: "How can you get home without reaching Third Base?" Once led by John F. Kennedy's grandfather, Boston mayor John "Honey Fitz" Fitzgerald, the Royal Rooters were credited by many Sox players with having won the 1903 World Series by putting Pittsburgh star Honus Wagner into a slump. Today, they arrive wearing loud red badges and flashing plenty of dollars at the New York fans. They are prepared to back their beloved team with more than music.

That is the final shock of our imaginary trip to the ballpark of 1904: Gambling is everywhere. Present-day fans can hardly comprehend how much open gambling there was in those days, both inside the ballpark and out, and how perfectly accepted it was. Baseball players betting on games—within certain limits, such as not betting on their own teams to lose—is tolerated, professional gamblers own and run teams, and respectable newspapers brag that the hometown fans put down the biggest wagers. The presence at today's game of Joseph "Sport" Sullivan, down from Boston, strikes an ominous note for no one but us, who know that fifteen years

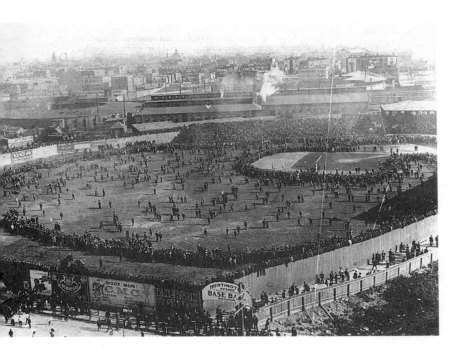

A panorama shot of Boston's Huntington Avenue Baseball Grounds prior to a 1903 World Series game. The AL Boston club upset the NL's Pittsburgh Pirates five games to three to win the first modern World Series.

from now, by some accounts to the very day, this underworld fixer and bookmaker will pay eight members of the Chicago "Black Sox" to throw the 1919 World Series. The ensuing scandal almost destroyed the major leagues and left organized baseball in a state of institutional paranoia about gambling that persists, as the Pete Rose affair attests, to present times.

The sudden, unexpected appearance of the sun at game time seemed just one more improbable bit of luck for the underdog Yankees, who—even their biggest fans had to concede—had no business taking player-manager Jimmy Collins and his defending world cham-

*Fans enjoy the deciding game of the
1903 World Series. During the dead-ball era,
most baseball fans were affluent white men whose
work schedule allowed them to attend the
late afternoon games.*

pions down to the last day of a pennant race. Collins,
the greatest third baseman of his era, and hard-hitting
center fielder Chick Stahl were the nucleus of a great
Boston Beaneaters dynasty that won NL flags in 1897
and 1898 before jumping across town to the newly
formed American League in 1901. They took with them
Buck Freeman, a top RBI-man and one of the few hitters
to reach double figures in home runs regularly in those
pre-Ruth days, and 1903 World Series hero Big Bill
Dineen. Dineen had won three games for the Red Sox
in their victory over the Pittsburgh Pirates in the first
World Series, which in its time rated as a national sen-

sation in the same class as the New York Jets' win over the Baltimore Colts in the 1969 Super Bowl. In that low-scoring era, the bunt, hit-and-run, and stolen base were the predominant offensive tactics. Boston had answers for all three; cannon-armed catcher Lou Criger, a state-of-the-art infield defense, and an awesome four-man pitching staff made up of Cy Young, still overpowering at age 37, Dineen, six-time 20-game winner Jesse Tannehill, and a fourth starter, Norwood Gibson, who won 17 games. This staff allowed an average of only 1.5 walks per nine innings pitched, still the lowest mark in history.

The Yankees, on the other hand, looked a lot more like an expansion team than a pennant contender. Chesbro was New York's only legitimate star. The rest of the team was an unremarkable mixture of youngish mediocrities and faded great names like 38-year-old catcher James "Deacon" McGuire; Wee Willie Keeler, a future Hall-of-Famer six years past his last batting title; and over-the-hill pitcher-manager Clark Griffith. Somehow this outfit managed to stay within 4½ games of the first-place Red Sox as late as June 18. On that date, Boston management showed just how lightly it took the Yankees when it sent its fleet leadoff man Patsy Dougherty to New York in a trade for back-up infielder Bob Unglaub and an amount of money not to be named later.

The Dougherty deal incensed the Boston fans. The erratic but talented Dougherty may have been in manager Collins's doghouse, but he had batted .331 and led the league in runs scored in 1903 and was the darling of the Royal Rooters. Popular anger over the trade—aimed at Boston owner John Taylor, the publisher of the *Boston Globe*—gave way to theorizing that American League president Ban Johnson was fixing the pennant race in New York's favor. Johnson's motive was supposed to be to stick it to longtime personal enemies

John Brush and John McGraw, the owner and manager respectively of the New York Giants, who were then running away with the NL flag. There were still plenty of hard feelings left over from Monopoly War IV, especially in New York where the Giants and Yankees were locked in a bitter local battle for the hearts and wallets of fans in baseball's biggest market.

It only rubbed salt in the Boston fans' wounds that in his first game wearing a New York uniform on June 25, Patsy Dougherty singled three times to beat Cy Young in Boston. He then went on a hitting tear and sparked a surge that cut the Yankees' deficit down to 1½ games. Unglaub got into only nine games for Boston that season and batted .154.

Dougherty and the Yankees hung tough through a series of injuries to regulars in June and July, and in late August they took the lead in what was then a five-team race. On August 27th, the standings were as follows:

New York	65–42	.608
Boston	66–43	.606
Philadelphia	60–44	.577
Chicago	64–47	.577
Cleveland	60–46	.566

Philadelphia, Chicago, and Cleveland soon dropped back, leaving New York and Boston to take turns in first place throughout September. The amazing thing about the New York pennant drive is that while Collins's stars remained healthy, the Yankees' bad luck with injuries turned even worse. Rookie Jack "Red" Kleinow had to take over all catching duties from a banged-up McGuire; several fingers smashed by pitches and an ugly spiking on the base paths sidelined Keeler for two different stretches; outfielder Davey Fultz was reported to be "over strained"—whatever that meant, he sat out the rest of the season—and offensive catalyst Dougherty came down with malaria! As for the pitchers, third starter Al "The Curveless Wonder" Orth blew out his pitching shoulder, and the 34-year-old Griffith became too tired even to take an occasional pitching turn. There was only one thing keeping the Yankees in the race: Jack Chesbro.

Chesbro, whose nickname "Happy Jack" was an ironic reference to his fierce demeanor on the mound, was a tough, thickly built right-hander with a reputation for enjoying a drink and a party. His crackling fastball, rated by many as second only to that of strikeout king Rube Waddell, and his willingness to use it to knock batters off the plate took him from the sandlots of his native western Massachusetts up the minor-league ladder, until in 1897 he reached Richmond of the highly competitive Atlantic League. It was probably there that Chesbro began to experiment with the newly invented spitball. With his huge hands and long fingers, Chesbro soon mastered the pitch and in 1899 joined the Pittsburgh Pirates, who were in the process of building the first great NL dynasty of this century. Not only was Chesbro a pioneer in the art of the spitter, but no pitcher then or since has thrown it harder or with better control. It is also doubtful that any threw a wetter "wet one" than Happy Jack; some contemporary observers felt that Chesbro's heavy loading up of the baseball explained the high number of infield errors that seemed to be made behind him. He came into his own in 1901, the year the AL opened for business, when he went 21–9, leading the league in both shutouts and winning percentage, for the first-place Pirates. In 1902 Chesbro went 28–6, again leading in winning percentage and shutouts, as Pittsburgh repeated.

That year the blossoming AL continued to lure away NL stars with offers of large contracts, and in the off-season the New York Yankees landed Chesbro, one of the biggest fish of all, for what was rumored to be the

New York Yankees pitcher "Happy" Jack Chesbro
limbers up his pitching arm during pregame warm-ups.
Chesbro was the goat of the 1904 AL pennant race,
won by the Boston Red Sox on the last day of the season.

greatest sum of money ever given a professional
ballplayer. This turned out to deprive Chesbro of an
opportunity to play in the first World Series in 1903. But
Jack Chesbro's situation in 1904 was more pressure-

filled than any World Series game. Plenty of free agents in today's game have faced what he faced, the agonizing responsibility of meeting the unreal fan and media expectations that often come along with a big free-agent contract, but Chesbro was carrying the fortunes of an entire league.

Ever since he had begun planning for a new major league in the 1890s, AL president Ban Johnson had known that a successful franchise in New York was the key. But with its toxic political climate dominated by the super-corrupt Tammany Hall machine, associates of which owned the New York Giants, the city had proven a tough nut to crack. For years, Johnson couldn't even find a suitable site for a ballpark; before the ink dried on his lease, he would find city agencies condemning the property, cutting new streets through it, and in one case, even diverting a new subway line so that fans would have no way of getting there. In 1903 Johnson finally decided to adopt the principle of "if you can't beat 'em, join 'em." As part of the compromise that settled the war between the AL and NL, Johnson sold the team to wealthy bookmaker and race horse owner Frank Farrell and even wealthier former New York City police commissioner Big Bill Devery, both of whom had solid Tammany connections. Devery's official style as chief of New York's Finest is captured by his famous motto: "If there's any graftin' to be done, I'm going to be the one that does it." As for Farrell, Frank Graham's history of the Yankees includes this exchange that took place during the first meeting between Farrell, go-between Joe Vila, and a somewhat naive Ban Johnson, who is unconvinced that Farrell is a man of sufficient financial substance to operate a baseball team:

> Farrell (flashing a certified check for $25,000): "Take that as a guarantee of good faith, Mr. Johnson. If I don't put this club across, keep it."

Johnson: "That's a pretty big forfeit, Mr. Farrell."
Vila: "He bets that much on one race, Ban."

Both Farrell and Chesbro came through as promised; in their first year the Yankees went 72–62 and came in a respectable fourth. Jack Chesbro went 21–15 with a 2.77 ERA, the same sort of performance he had given Pittsburgh, but his best was yet to come.

Chesbro opened the 1904 season as the Yankees' staff ace and took on an ever-increasing share of the burden, first Griffith's starts and then Orth's, until in the final weeks of the pennant race he seemed to be carrying the entire Yankees team on his broad shoulders. Adding to his workload was the fact that in 1904 the AL expanded its schedule from 140 games to 154. From April through August the stout right-hander started 36 games and completed 35. Then came September and October, when Chesbro made an unbelievable 15 starts in less than a month and a half, going the distance in 13, and won some of the biggest games of the season. On September 16 he beat the Red Sox and Big Bill Dineen by a score of 6-4, and in a double-header with Boston four days later he replaced the injured Orth in the tenth inning of game one, won the game 3-2, then started and won the nightcap 5-1. The Red Sox won nearly all their other games in late September and into early October, but Happy Jack's victories over Chicago on October 1 and St. Louis on October 3 kept the Yankees close. After the games of the fifth of October, the American League race was a virtual dead heat. With one five-game series left to play between the two contenders in New York, the standings were:

Boston	92–57	.617
New York	90–56	.616

On Friday October 7th, Jack Chesbro scattered four hits and beat Boston again, 3-2. The Yankees now held the lead in the closest race in major-league baseball's 30-year history by six percentage points and could clinch the pennant merely by splitting the remaining four games with Boston.

Next comes an infuriating turn in the plot that vividly demonstrates how much less seriously major-league baseball took itself in those days before concrete-and-steel ballparks, millionaire players, and ESPN. On Saturday October 8, the schedule called for a doubleheader between Boston and the Yankees at New York's Hilltop Park. A few months earlier, however, Yankees co-owner Frank Farrell, perhaps never dreaming that his team would still be in the race, had rented the park on that date for a college football game between Columbia and Williams. The baseball games were transferred to Boston, where the Yankees promptly dropped them both. The Red Sox now led by a game and a half with two to play; Griffith's weary team returned home on Sunday needing to sweep a season-ending doubleheader the following day to win the pennant.

As the one o'clock starting time for the big double-header approached, tensions built on both sides of the foul lines. Chesbro would pitch for New York and Dineen for Boston. A cheering battle broke out between the Royal Rooters with their music on one side and the masses of Yankees fans, armed only with cardboard megaphones, on the other. As if any more pressure was needed, in recent days it had become clear that the New York Giants would refuse to play the AL champions in a postseason series in 1904. For weeks, new Giants owner and longtime Ban Johnson nemesis John Brush, along with his manager John McGraw, had engaged in a public spitting contest with Johnson and the Yankees over the issue. Brush issued a statement calling the American League a minor league and declaring the Giants satisfied to rest on their National

League laurels. Referring to a financial dispute between himself and Johnson that dated back to McGraw's days with the AL Baltimore Orioles, McGraw snarled, "I know the American League and its methods. I ought to, for they still have my money." Everybody knew the real reason the Giants didn't want to play; they were simply afraid the rival Yankees might win the pennant and then beat them in the postseason. A series of pointed public challenges from both the Yankees and Red Sox, a petition signed by 10,000 New Yorkers, and even $50,000 in cash put up by a bookmaking syndicate could not change the Giants' minds. As every one of the 28,584 fans waiting for the start of the game knew, this season the pennant race was it. There would be nothing more to win.

Through four scoreless innings neither pitcher betrayed any sign of nervousness. Chesbro seemed particularly loose. Before his at-bat in the third inning, the game was briefly halted so that a delegation of fans could present him with a fur coat in honor of his 41 wins; Chesbro responded by smacking a line drive into the right field corner and sprinting all the way to third waving his cap to the cheering crowd. Then in the fifth Dineen faltered, allowing a pair of runs on singles by Kleinow, Chesbro, and Dougherty followed by two bases on balls. Each call of "ball four" was met with derisive choruses of "Tessie" from the hometown fans. The score remained 2-0 until the seventh, when Yankees second baseman Jimmy Williams, who according to one newspaper reporter looked "a bit worried by the responsibility of the contest," booted a grounder to put one runner on base and one out later allowed two to score on a wild throw to the plate. Boston should have won the game in the eighth, but Chick Stahl somehow failed to score from second on a double over the centerfielder's head and the game went into the top of the ninth tied 2-2. Lou Criger led off for Boston and reached base on an infield bloop. The slow-footed catcher advanced to second on Dineen's sacrifice and reached third on the second out, a grounder to shortstop Kid Elberfeld. Chesbro got two quick strikes on the next batter, shortstop Freddy Parent, and then threw the pitch that, according to his obituary, "above everything else, made [him] famous."

Eyewitnesses differ on how wild Chesbro's 0-2 waste pitch really was. Some describe it as a shoulder-high fastball up and away from the right-hand-hitting Parent; others say that it was a spitter that broke 10 feet; still others claim that the pitch struck the grandstand on the fly—a distance of more than 150 feet! Kid Elberfeld wins the exaggeration contest for telling Fred Lieb of *The Sporting News* in 1942 that "the ball went so far over Jack [Kleinow]'s head that he couldn't have reached it with a crab net." All versions agree, however, that it was correctly scored a wild pitch. Chesbro then gave up a hit to Parent before recording the final out. In the bottom of the ninth Dineen made it interesting by walking two with two out, but Boston fan favorite Patsy Dougherty, of all people, struck out to give Boston the pennant. The Yankees won the meaningless second game, 1-0, before a considerably smaller and nearly silent crowd.

THE YEAR: 1904

AL fans enjoyed the first of many Boston–New York pennant races in 1904, thanks mainly to Yankees pitcher Jack Chesbro's record 41 wins, 51 starts, and 48 complete games. None of this, however, saved Chesbro from becoming one of the all-time pennant-race goats when he wild-pitched in the pennant-losing run on the last day of the season.

Fourth-place Cleveland had the league's best offense in 1904. The great Lajoie banged out 50 doubles and batted .381 to win another batting title; he also led the AL in both on-base average and slugging average. Teammate Elmer Flick scored 97 runs, hit 17 triples, and collected 262 total bases. Cleveland pitcher Adrian "Addie" Joss took the ERA title at 1.59, the first of his amazing five sub-2.00 ERA seasons.

Philadelphia flamethrower Rube Waddell struck out 349 men at a very modern-looking rate of 8.2 per nine innings; the AL runner-up in Ks, Chesbro, struck out 110 fewer despite pitching 72 more innings. Waddell's 1904 strikeout total is the fourth-best ever; every other season on the top 10 list came in the strikeout-happy post–World War II era.

John McGraw won his first NL pennant in grand style; his Giants won a record 106 games and lost only 47. The pitching was ably handled by workhorses McGinnity and Mathewson, who won 68 games between them. A typical McGraw team, New York led the NL in offense, the result of a complete team effort. Lacking a dominant star, the Giants lineup was made up of beautifully complementary parts, including right fielder George Browne, who led the league in runs with 99, shortstop Bill Dahlen, who led in RBIs with 80, and left fielder Sam Mertes, who was second in doubles with 28. As a team, the Giants led the league in runs, hits, doubles, home runs, walks, batting average, and stolen bases. McGinnity won the National League ERA title at 1.61, the finest seasonal ERA of his long, Hall-of-Fame career.

The Pirates were let down by poor pitching and finished fourth; Wagner won his third batting title and stole a league-leading 53 bases. Frank Selee, the architect of Boston's 1890s dynasty, was now engaged in rebuilding the once-glorious Chicago Cubs franchise. In 1904 he led second-place Chicago to 93 wins with a young team made up of future stars Frank Chance, Johnny Evers (pronounced "Ee'-vers", not "Ev'-vers"), and Joe Tinker; the Cubs would be heard from soon.

Fans who anticipated another exciting interleague postseason series were disappointed when John McGraw and New York owner John Brush issued a late-season press release stating that they would refuse to meet the AL pennant winner.

What happened to Jack Chesbro? The big right-hander seems to have accepted his fate as philosophically as could be expected. He would never say much on the subject, beyond refusing to deny responsibility for the wild pitch and saying that such things were "all part of the game." After all, there were plenty of reasons not to blame him alone for the Yankees' loss. There were Williams's errors, Dougherty's strikeout, and—to some—catcher Kleinow's slowness in retrieving both Chesbro's wild pitch and Williams's seventh-inning throw in the dirt. Many blamed manager Griffith for overworking Chesbro down the stretch, which he undeniably did, or pointed to the obvious fact that without Chesbro, the Yankees would never have been within 10 games of first place, let alone one and a half. But unfairly or not, Jack Chesbro soon discovered his error was all anybody seemed to want to remember about the 1904 pennant race. As the story was told and retold, it was hyped by the newspapers to ever greater heights of melodrama, and the name Chesbro became synonymous with big-time failure for an entire generation of fans.

As the years passed by, despite efforts by friends to shift the blame to Kleinow by attacking the official scorer's decision, Jack Chesbro became the first modern baseball goat. His wild pitch became the standard by which all other clutch foul-ups were measured. Happy Jack's example was trotted out in 1907 when Wild Bill Donovan's pitch got by Charley Schmidt in the World Series, in 1908 when Ed Walsh (also a spitballer), threw a wild pitch that scored the pennant-losing run on the last day of the season, when John "Chief" Meyers failed

52

to handle a pitch in the 1911 Series, and even as late as 1927, when Pirates pitcher John Miljus wild-pitched home a Yankees runner with the series-deciding run. Chesbro's misfortune set a pattern whose basic elements have been shared by nearly all goat stories since. He was the kind of star who is supposed to come through in the clutch but didn't; his wild pitch had a farcical element lacking in garden-variety errors like those of Williams; and it came in the biggest game of the year. There is one more essential aspect to Chesbro's goathood: the fact that he played in New York, the city that would later give us renowned goats Merkle, Snodgrass, Owen, and Branca. Just as it has made so many larger-than-life heroes—and for many of the same reasons—the New York sports scene, with its unique mixture of ill will, bad sportsmanship, media intensity, and, of course, abundant pennant races and World Series, has always been fertile ground for the creation of goats.

During the winter of 1904–05, Jack Chesbro told an interviewer that because the spitball was so easy on the arm, he expected no ill effects from throwing 455 innings the previous season. He could not have been more wrong. His workload fell in the next few seasons to the 300-inning range, and his arm never did snap back. Nineteen-hundred-and-six was his last winning season, and by 1909 he had left the big leagues to return to his chicken farm in the Berkshires. There he died in 1931 at the age of 56. Ten years later, as part of a campaign to put Chesbro into the Hall of Fame, his widow and a number of friends reopened the phony issue of whether the official scorer should have ruled Chesbro's wild pitch a passed ball instead. This was as futile as it was unnecessary. By this time, the 1904 pennant race had faded from popular memory. When Brooklyn Dodgers catcher Mickey Owen lost the 1941 World Series to the New York Yankees by letting Hugh

53

Casey's two-strike, two-out, ninth-inning spitball get past him, not one New York paper picked up on the obvious parallels to the Jack Chesbro story.

There is, however, one part of baseball's past that does not fade: the statistical record. Chesbro's 41 wins, 51 games started, and 48 complete games remain 20th-century records; his 455 innings pitched is second only to fellow dead-ball era spitballer Ed Walsh's 464 in 1908. It is thanks to these records that Happy Jack was named to the Hall of Fame in 1946 and has finally gotten his due for the great deeds of 1904. Some argue that Chesbro's 1904 numbers are overrated because the record books arbitrarily divide the 20th century from the 19th, when many pitchers won more games and threw more innings than Chesbro. It is also true that he pitched in freakish and unrepeatable conditions, such as the terrible pressure on manager Griffith and the Yankees to win that particular pennant, the widespread false belief that the spitball put almost no strain on the pitching arm, and uncertainty over how the foul-strike rule and the 154-game schedule would affect pitchers' workloads. Even so, it is fitting that Chesbro should finally be known for his undeniably Herculean one-man pitching show, rather than for one bad pitch. They may be overrated, but until baseball adopts a 200-game schedule, or changes its rules to create a new dead-ball era, Happy Jack's 1904 records will live forever.

Big Six, the Cyclone, and the Big Train: A Generation of Pitching Heroes

Jack Chesbro is not the only pitcher of the 1900s and 1910s whose name lives on in the pitching section of the baseball record book. In fact, most major all-time pitching records are monopolized by members of two baseball generations: the pitchers of the dead-ball era and pitchers who began their careers in the middle 1960s. Take the list of the pitchers with 300 or more lifetime wins. Most fans today know all about Steve Carlton (pitched 1965–88), Don Sutton (1966–88), Nolan Ryan (1966–92), Phil Niekro (1965–87), Gaylord Perry (1963–83), and Tom Seaver (1967–86). Few, however, know more than the names of the dead-ball era pitchers who make up nearly all of the rest of the list: Cy Young (1890–1911), Walter Johnson (1907–27), Grover Cleveland "Pete" Alexander (1911–30), Christy Mathewson (1900–16), and Eddie Plank (1901–17). Even if we set aside Alexander, who pitched half of his career after the dead-ball era in the 1920s, and Plank, who does not belong in the same class as the rest of the group, it can be argued that the three greatest dead-ball pitchers—Young, Johnson, and Mathewson—are the three greatest pitchers ever. Certainly, with 1301 career wins among them, this trio dominated their time in a way that no other group of pitching stars have before or since.

Denton True "Cy" Young was rarely the best pitcher in his league in any given season. For most of his career he did not have eye-popping statistics or a dominating fastball; he gave up around a hit an inning and struck out about one batter every other inning—figures that would earn most modern pitchers a trip back to the minor leagues. There is, however, a very good reason why each season the best pitcher in each league is given an award named after Cy Young: He was the winningest, most consistent, and most durable pitcher who ever lived.

Most pitchers and pitching coaches will tell you that successful pitching is all about making adjustments. Over the course of his career, Cy Young had to adjust to some of the greatest changes that baseball has gone through. When he came up in 1890, pitchers worked out of a box, releasing the ball with their back foot touching a line 55½ feet from home plate; when he retired in 1911 pitchers were throwing from a pitching rubber atop a mound, five feet farther away from the batter. And Cy Young's career is neatly divided in half by the foul-strike rule, which ended one of baseball's highest-scoring eras ever and brought on two decades of dead ball.

Throughout all of these changes, Young remained, year in and year out, one of baseball's top three or four pitchers. He averaged 27 wins and 15 losses a year with a 3.05 ERA in the 1890s and an identical 27–15, with an ERA of 2.12, in the 1900s. Seeming never to get a sore arm, Young set a series of longevity records that remain unapproached. He started 815 games, the most all-time; completed 749, also the most all-time; and threw 7,377 innings, more than a thousand more than 19th-century great James "Pud" Galvin, who is second on the all-time list. He won over 200 games in both the NL and the AL for an incredible career total of 511—or, as Young liked to say to anyone who asked him how many games he had won: "more than you'll ever see."

How did Cy Young pitch so well for so long? Part of the answer is stuff and part of it is control. Early in his career, Young got hitters out with speed and little else. Nicknamed "Cy" because his fastball seemed as fast as a cyclone, he disdained breaking pitches, which he termed "junk," particularly that staple of modern pitching, the slider, which he dismissed as a "nickel curve." When asked if he ever changed speeds, Young would say, "yes: fast, faster, and fastest." Young's pride in his velocity was such that as long as he lived, until 1955, he never admitted to seeing a major-league pitcher who threw harder. That included the legendary Cleveland Indians fireballer Bob Feller, whom Young often traveled from his Ohio farm to see during the 1930s and 1940s. Few opposing hitters, however, considered Young to be a hard thrower in the same class as an Amos Rusie or a Walter Johnson. And age took its toll on Young's fastball; by the early 1900s he was keeping hitters honest with an excellent curve thrown from a bewildering variety of arm angles and an assortment of other "junk." Toward the end of his career he was even accused of resorting to the spitball.

Cy Young's real forte was control. It may not have been so difficult to get a hit here and there off Young, but he did not walk *anybody*. He issued a little over 1,200 bases on balls in more than 7,300 innings—an average of fewer than 1.5 walks per nine innings—and led his league in fewest walks per nine innings in a season an incredible 11 times. It was not that Young could not crank it up a notch when he wanted to; at 37, he fired a perfect game against strikeout artist Rube

Waddell after Waddell had publicly vowed that he would one-hit Young and the Red Sox. "I figured he was calling me out," said Young after the game, "and I had better do something about it." But keeping men off base, not overpowering them, was the key to consistent success in dead-ball–style baseball. Although Young only led the league in ERA and strikeouts twice each, he held opposing batters to the lowest on-base average (hits plus walks per plate appearance) in eight different seasons. For his 22-year career, major-league hitters batted a collective .252 with a .287 OBA against Cy Young, or about as well as a modern utility infielder. Even pitching half his career in the run-happy 1890s, Cy Young turned opposing lineups that boasted the likes of Wee Willie Keeler, Ed Delahanty, John McGraw, Larry Lajoie, Ty Cobb, and Honus Wagner into nine Alvaro Espinozas.

The real mystery of Cy Young is how he lasted so long with his quirky views on physical conditioning. From his major-league debut, a victory over the Chicago White Stockings that led Cap Anson to offer a wad of cash for the young pitcher on the spot, to his final appearance as a pudgy old man with the Boston Braves in 1911, Young never worked out, in-season or off. The best exercise for a pitcher, he explained, was the wood chopping and rail splitting that occupied Young on his farm during the winter months. The rest of the time Young was fanatical about conserving his arm strength. He refused to throw between starts, took it easy in spring training, and warmed up as little as possible; he even disliked throwing to first base with a runner on, feeling that he was wasting pitches that might be better used against a batter. As eccentric as Young's theories may sound, it is hard to argue with the results. When he retired in his mid-forties, Young said that his arm was feeling fine—he had thrown two shutouts in 11 starts that season—it was just that he was too fat and slow to field his position and opposing hitters were bunting him out of the game.

THE YEAR: 1905

Dead ball was never deader than in the American League in 1905, a year in which only two men, Wee Willie Keeler and Elmer Flick, batted over .300. Flick won the AL batting title by hitting only .306, the lowest average to lead either league until Carl Yastrzemski's .301 in 1968. The entire AL batted only .241. On the pitching side, all eight teams had ERAs under 3.00, and Rube Waddell won the ERA title at 1.48. The next four pitchers on the ERA list, Guy "Doc" White, Cy Young, Andy Coakley, and Nick Altrock, were all under 1.89. Of the all-time top 20 pitchers in lifetime ERA, 15 pitched in 1905.

Three of the top 20—Waddell, Chief Bender, and Eddie Plank—were pitching for the Philadelphia Athletics, who fought a long, grueling battle with Chicago to win the pennant by two games. Rube Waddell pitched 44 consecutive scoreless innings down the stretch in September and led the league in wins, strikeouts, and ERA. The White Sox' pitching was actually better on paper, with Frank Owen, Nick Altrock, Frank Smith, and Doc White, who combined for a staff ERA of 1.99. Chicago's fifth starter was spitball specialist Ed Walsh, who went on to record the lowest career ERA in history, 1.82. The Athletics held a slight advantage over Chicago thanks to a versatile offense of Harry Davis, who led the AL in runs scored with 92, RBIs with 83,and doubles with 47; 77-RBI man Lave Cross; and run-scoring virtuoso Topsy Hartsel, who drew an AL-high 121 bases on balls.

Elmer Flick led the league in triples with 19 and slugging average at .466, but Cleveland faded to fifth after Larry Lajoie's season was cut short by a bad spiking that led to a case of blood poisoning. In Detroit, the Tigers climbed out of the second division to claim third place thanks to strong seasons from several talented youngsters. George Mullin and Ed Killian won over 20 games, and 25-year-old Sam Crawford was fourth in hitting at .297 and second in doubles with 40. Eighteen-year-old Ty Cobb was called up in late August, played 41 games, and batted .240—the first and last time he would hit below .300 in 24 major-league seasons.

The National League race was over on April 23, when McGraw's defending champions took over first place for good; the Giants won 105 games to finish well ahead of Pittsburgh and Chicago. Led by the underrated hard thrower Ed Reulbach, the Cubs had four pitchers among the top five in ERA, but New York's combination of Mathewson, McGinnity, and Leon "Red" Ames on the mound and .356-hitting Mike Donlin at the plate proved unbeatable.

How dead was the dead-ball era? With an ERA of 3.21, a figure that would lead a modern league in some years, Vic Willis lost 29 games, the most in modern history, for seventh-place Boston. The immortal Cy Young somehow went 18–19 on an ERA of 1.82.

It is perhaps no surprise that the 1905 World Series was the best-pitched series ever; all five games were shutouts and the losers, Philadelphia, had an ERA of 1.47. It was also one of the most one-sided. Behind Christy Mathewson's three shutouts and 15 base runners allowed in 27 innings, New York took the series by a composite score of 15-3. The Giants' team ERA for the series was a perfect 0.00.

If Cy Young was the winningest pitcher in the dead-ball years, the New York Giants' Christy Mathewson was the era's greatest hero. A blue-eyed, fair-haired college graduate in a time when baseball players ranked somewhere below sailors and actors in social

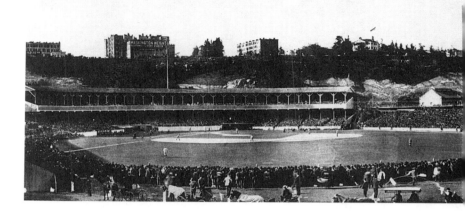

The New York Giants host the Philadelphia A's in the 1905 World Series.

standing, he was revered by teammates and fans alike for his grace, gentlemanliness, and sense of sportsmanship. Called Matty or Big Six, after a champion New York City volunteer fire company of the 19th century, Mathewson was so known for his integrity that during games umpires would sometimes ask him for help on a close call on the bases. Remembering Mathewson years later, Giants catcher Chief Meyers said,

> *How we loved to play for him! We'd break our necks for that guy. If you made an error behind him, or anything of that sort, he'd never get mad or sulk. He'd come over and pat you on the back. He had the sweetest, most gentle nature. Gentle in every way. He was a great checker player, too. He'd play several men at once. Actually, that's what made him a great pitcher.*

New York Giants ace pitcher, Christy Mathewson

His wonderful retentive memory. Any time you hit a ball hard off him, you never got another pitch in that spot again.[1]

During his lifetime and especially after his untimely death in 1925, Mathewson's image as a gentleman athlete out of a prep school novel, who never drank, gambled, or played baseball on Sunday, was played up to the point of exaggeration. In a newspaper interview after his death, Mathewson's widow, Jane, felt it necessary to explain that her husband had been a fine man, but "no goody-goody."

Certainly, it is hard to imagine the moral paragon that Mathewson was often held up to be becoming personally close to John McGraw. In fact, McGraw, the rough, even crude, son of an Irish immigrant railroad worker, and Mathewson, the educated child of middle-class English immigrants, were the best and strongest of friends. Like McGraw, Mathewson showed plenty of guts on and off the field. In an era with a high tolerance for corruption, Mathewson was one of the few to stand up and demand that something be done about the crooked but immensely popular first baseman Hal Chase. Chase instigated many of the gambling and game-fixing scandals that marred baseball in the 1910s and played a behind-the-scenes role in the infamous Black Sox scandal of 1919.

Mathewson's story is typical of a pitcher with more intelligence and courage than pure stuff. Armed with a good fastball and a slow, wide-breaking curve that gave major-league hitters little trouble, the right-handed Mathewson was sent down to the minors after going 0–3 with a 5.08 ERA in 1900, his rookie season. But he quickly learned his lesson; he returned the following year to go 20–17 and blossomed after John McGraw took over as Giants manager in 1902. From 1903 to 1914, Mathewson won 20 or more games every year and 30 or more four times. He had learned to complement his fastball with a sharp curve and a new trick pitch called the fadeaway. Thrown with the same arm angle as his other pitches but breaking down and away from lefthanded hitters, Mathewson's fadeaway was almost certainly the modern screwball. Like Cy Young and his fellow dead-ball era pitching masters, Mathewson had learned how to pitch smart, relying on his defense, and how to outthink opposing hitters. Writing, as he often did, in a parody of contemporary ballplayer slang, sports columnist Ring Lardner described the Giants right-hander as follows:

> *There's a flock o' pitchers that knows a batter's weakness and works accordin'. But they ain't nobody else in the world that can stick a ball as near where they want to stick it as he can. I bet he could shave you if he wanted to and if he had a razor blade to throw instead of a ball. If you can't hit a fast one a inch and a quarter inside and he knows it, you'll get three fast ones a inch and a quarter inside, and then, if you've swung at 'em you can go get a drink o' water.*[2]

Christy Mathewson won 373 games in his 17 years in the majors, third-best all-time, and compiled a career ERA of 2.13, fourth-best among 20th-century pitchers. He prided himself on rising to the occasion in big games, and, playing with McGraw's Giants, there was no shortage of pennant races and World Series to provide a national stage for Mathewson's heroics. His career was marked by a series of wonderful pitching duels against Mordecai "Three Finger" Brown of the archrival Chicago Cubs. Not only did Matty personally dominate the 1905 World Series, but in 101 postseason innings he allowed only 76 hits and 10 walks, compiling an ERA of 1.15.

Christy Mathewson's life came to a tragic end in 1925 when he died at the age of 45 of tuberculosis. He had contracted the disease after a training accident involving poison gas that occurred while he was serving with the U.S. Army in France during World War I. Besides his many records and accomplishments, Mathewson left behind a book, called *Pitching in a Pinch*, that offers a unique inside look into baseball in the pre–home run era. In the book, Mathewson describes how the best pitchers pace themselves until the critical moments, late in a game, when they need to use their best stuff to stop a big inning by the opposition. Called "pinches" by Mathewson, these moments are what we usually call "the clutch" today. "In most big league ball games," Mathewson writes, "there comes an inning on which hangs victory or defeat. . . . This is the time when each team is straining every nerve either to win or to prevent defeat. . . . It is at this moment that [the pitcher] is 'putting all he has' on the ball."[3]

Christy Mathewson certainly practiced what he preached; he was known for holding back a few nasty screwballs or his best fastball in order to squelch a late-inning rally. The interesting thing about reading Mathewson's book today is that while we still speak of "clutch" hitting, in modern, home-run oriented baseball there is no longer such a thing as pitching in the "pinch" or "clutch." The reason for this is that, with lively baseballs, small ballparks, and even the lightest hitters capable of uppercutting one into the second deck, pitchers no longer have the luxury of easing back and waiting for the right moment to use their best stuff. If they do not throw as hard as they can for as long as they can, they will be long-balled into oblivion. In a sense, today's pitchers are always "pitching in a pinch."

THE YEAR: 1906

The 1906 season brought the first one-city World Series; over the next 83 years there would be 14 more—13 played in New York City—but the '06 series was unique. It was baseball's first, last, and only all-Chicago affair.

In early June, first baseman–manager Frank Chance's Cubs powerhouse kicked off the greatest run of success by any NL dynasty of the 1900s by setting a still-standing major-league record of 116 regular-season wins—including 60 on the road, also a record—against only 36 losses. The steady Chance led the way for an offense that outscored its nearest rival by 80 runs; he tied Honus Wagner for the league lead in runs scored with 103 and on-base average at .406. He also anchored the NL's top defensive infield, made up of third baseman and RBI-man Harry Steinfeldt and the immortal pair of shortstop Joe Tinker and second baseman Johnny Evers. This was the double-play combination made famous by Franklin P. Adams's poem, "Baseball's Sad Lexicon," published in the *New York Evening Mail* in 1910, which begins with the lines: "These are the saddest of possible words / Tinker to Evers to Chance." Chicago Cubs pitchers allowed only 381 runs, 89 fewer than the nearest team, and an incredible four of their five starters—Three Finger Brown, Ed Reulbach, Jack Pfiester, and Orval "Orvie" Overall—had ERAs below 2.00; Brown's ERA of 1.04 is the second-lowest ever. The Cubs finished 20 games ahead of the poor Giants, who are one of the few major-league teams in any era to win 96 games without ever really being in the race.

Chicago's entry in the AL race had a slightly tougher time of it, especially early in the season, when they found themselves bringing up the rear of a four-team race with Philadelphia, New York, and Cleveland. Then, in early August, the White Sox reeled off 19 straight victories to secure the pennant. The White Sox may not have lit up the scoreboard like their West Side counterparts, but their offense—which produced 570 runs, third-most in the league—hardly deserved its nickname, the Hitless Wonders. The Sox' nickname may reflect more the fact that Chicago had no conspicuous batting stars or sluggers to compare with St. Louis's George Stone, the league-leader in batting at .358 and slugging at .501, or Cleveland's Elmer Flick, who knocked out 34 doubles and a league-high 22 triples. The Sox had hit only seven home runs all season, and four regulars batted .230 or lower. Slugging, however, was not the name of the game in the deadball era. Center fielder–manager Fielder Jones's White Sox scratched out their runs by drawing walks (outfielders Jones and Ed Hahn were second and third, respectively, in the AL in walks), and working an aggressive running game; both second baseman Frank Isbell and first baseman Jiggs Donahue were in the top five in stolen bases. Chicago's only big RBI-man was a shortstop, George Davis, who drove in 80 runs, third-best in the league behind Lajoie and Philadelphia slugger Harry Davis.

With George Davis knocked out of the series by an injury, the American Leaguers entered the World Series distinct underdogs. It was only in the area of pitching that some contemporary observers considered the White Sox to be competitive with the Cubs. But in spite of the presence of Doc White, who won the AL ERA title at 1.52, and Ed Walsh, the author of a league-leading 10 shutouts, the Sox' pitching was generally rated no better than even with the Cubs'.

Because of frigid, snowy October weather in Chicago, runs were hard to come by in games one through four of the World Series. Altrock beat the Cubs 2-1 in the opener, played in the Cubs' West Side Grounds, and Walsh won game three 3-0, but the series was tied 2-2 going into the fifth game. Suddenly, however, the Hitless Wonders' bats caught fire, and they knocked around Reulbach to win, 8-6. The Sox shelled Cubs ace Three Finger Brown and Orvie Overall to take the deciding game by a score of 8-3. For the series, the White Sox narrowly outhit their opponents, .198 to .196, but decisively bettered the mighty Cubs in ERA, 1.50 to 3.40.

Every baseball generation produces one man who fans swear is the fastest pitcher who ever lived. In the 1890s it was Amos Rusie, "The Hoosier Thunderbolt";

in the 1940s it was Bob "Rapid Robert" Feller; in the 1970s it was the "Nolan Ryan Express"; today it is Randy "The Big Unit" Johnson. In the dead-ball era, it was Walter "The Big Train" Johnson.

Johnson's fastball was so impressive that exaggeration became inevitable. It is impossible to believe half of the things that were written or said about it; in fact, almost every baseball story ever told about a pitcher with great velocity has been told before about Walter Johnson. There is the anecdote about Cleveland's Ray Chapman walking back to the dugout after taking strike two from Johnson. When the umpire reminded him that he had one strike left, Chapman replied: "You can have it. It won't do me any good." Or Frank "Ping" Bodie's famous line: "You can't hit what you can't see." Finally, there is the classic about the hitter who brings a lantern to the plate during the late innings of a game that is in danger of being called on account of darkness. "Do you think," says the umpire, "that's going to help you see the ball?" To which the batter answers: "I ain't worried about that. I just want to make sure the Big Train can see me."

Looking at photographs of Walter Johnson pitching, it is easy to be skeptical that he threw anywhere near as hard as some of today's fireballers. For one thing, he threw with a sidearm, flinging delivery that resembled a man playing handball. This may have made it difficult for right-handed batters to pick up Johnson's pitches, but in the words of baseball historian Bill James, "If you threw a 90 MPH fastball with that motion, your arm would come off." Whatever it would have registered on a modern radar gun, however, there is no question that Johnson's fastball *looked* plenty fast from the perspective of the batter's box. Ty Cobb recalled the first time he faced Johnson, "a tall, shambling galoot of about twenty with arms so long they hung out of his sleeves and with a side-arm delivery that looked unimpressive

Walter Johnson, nicknamed "Big Train" because of his blazing fastball, was the most overpowering pitcher of the dead-ball era. Of his 416 career wins, 110 were shutouts.

at first glance." This was in 1907, when Johnson was a rookie, fresh from the semipro Idaho State League. "I watched him take that easy windup," Cobb said, "and then something went past me that made me flinch. The thing just hissed with danger."[4] Cobb was not the last AL hitter to learn to fear the Walter Johnson fastball. In his 20-year career with the Washington Senators, Johnson won 416 games, second only to Cy Young, led the league in strikeouts an amazing twelve times, including eight seasons in a row, and set a lifetime strikeout record of 3,508 that stood for more than half a century until it was broken by Nolan Ryan.

Walter Johnson's accomplishments are even more impressive when you consider that he spent most of his career pitching for losing clubs. Cy Young won more games and Christy Mathewson pitched far more big games, but no dead-ball era pitcher was more consistently overpowering than Johnson. On a better team, he may well have outshone both Young and Mathewson. For example, 110 of his lifetime victories were shutouts and he won 38 games by a score of 1-0; on the other hand, in 65 of his losses his teammates were shut out and in 26 of them they scored only one run. Johnson appeared in two World Series, but both were in the middle 1920s when he was well past his prime. Still, he managed to play the hero in Washington's 1924 World Championship by coming into game seven in relief and holding the New York Giants scoreless for four innings until Earl McNeely's bad-hop ground ball over Fred Lindstrom's head drove in the series-winning run.

THE YEAR: 1907

When Hughie Jennings, formerly the shortstop for the famed Baltimore Orioles dynasty of the 1890s, took over for Bill Armour as manager of the Detroit Tigers, the first thing he did was to move the young Ty Cobb from the bench into the everyday lineup. Almost by itself, this move was responsible for the Tigers' 21-game climb in the standings from sixth place in 1906 to first in 1907.

With Cobb batting behind him in the cleanup slot, Sam Crawford hit .323 and slugged .460, both second in the league, scored an AL-high 102 runs and knocked 34 doubles and 17 triples. All summer long, Cobb drove in Crawford and leadoff man Davy Jones, who scored 102 runs, and the Detroit offense tallied 694 runs, 89 more than the also-ran Yankees. Cobb himself drove in 116 runs, collected 212 hits, and stole 49 bases, all league-leading figures; he also led in batting at .350 and slugging at .473. With this kind of run support, Detroit's mediocre pitching staff of Ed Killian, George Mullin, and Wild Bill Donovan was good enough to beat out Philadelphia in a close race. Donovan had a decent ERA of 2.19, but thanks to outstanding run support compiled a 25–4 record; his .862 winning percentage is the tenth-best in history. The defending champion White Sox put up almost the same numbers as 1906, scoring the third-most runs in the league and allowing the fewest, but in the Year of Cobb they added up to no better than a close third-place finish.

Attracting little notice at the time was the debut with last-place Washington of a green young fastball pitcher named Walter Johnson, who went 5-9 with a 1.87 ERA and 5.53 strikeouts per game, a ratio exceeded only by the A's Rube Waddell.

The NL race could be summed up in one word: Chicago. Frank Chance's juggernaut slumped to 107 wins, but still finished 17 games in front of a Pittsburgh team that featured the NL's best offense. A resurgent Honus Wagner won his fifth batting title at .350 and led the league in doubles, stolen bases, on-base average, and slugging. Without a single hitter over .300, the Chicago attack slipped by more than a hundred runs, but the Cubs pitchers continued their utter domination of NL hitters. Led by Jack Pfiester's league-best 1.15 ERA, the fifth-lowest in history, and Carl Lundgren's 1.17 ERA, the eighth-best ever, Chicago pitchers occupied four of the top five spots on the ERA leader board. Every member of the five-man staff compiled an ERA under 2.00, and together they allowed a meager 370 runs, 11 fewer than in 1906.

Giants catcher Roger Bresnahan became the first receiver to wear shin guards and a face mask during a game. This enabled him to survive an unprecedented 234 games behind the plate in 1907 and 1908.

The World Series was a mismatch, with Detroit managing only a first-game 3-3 tie out of the five games played. For the remainder of the series, the Tigers never scored more than one run in a single game, as the Chicago staff posted a composite ERA of 0.75. Cobb and Crawford batted only .200 and .238 and managed only a pair of extra-base hits between them, but the biggest surprise of the series was that Cobb was shut out on the base paths by rifle-armed Chicago catcher Johnny Kling. Led by Jimmy Slagle's six stolen bases, the Cubs outstole the Tigers 16-6.

Off the field, Albert Spalding's blue-ribbon panel, the Mills Commission, published the results of its so-called investigation into the origins of baseball, a laughable document that purported to prove that Civil War hero Abner Doubleday had invented the game in the rural village of Cooperstown, New York, in 1839. In reality, Doubleday had no known connection to the game at all. The first baseball club with formal rules and a regular organization was the New York Knickerbocker Club, which was founded in the early 1840s by a group of Wall Street bank clerks and shopkeepers. The Mills Commission report inspired the opening of the National Baseball Hall of Fame in Cooperstown in 1939.

CHAPTER FOUR

Touching Second: The Merkle Blunder and the Greatest Pennant Races Ever

The greatest pennant race of the dead-ball era, if not the greatest pennant race ever, was the summerlong dogfight for the NL flag in 1908. Strangely enough, the second-greatest pennant race took place in that same year, in the American League. Both races came down to the final day of the season; both ended with three clubs separated in the standings by one game or less. To non-baseball fans, 1908 was the year that nobody talked about the presidential election until November.

The events of 1908 figure prominently in interviews, memoirs, and biographies of such great dead-ball-era stars as Three Finger Brown, Johnny Evers, John McGraw, Christy Mathewson, Honus Wagner, Ty Cobb, Larry Lajoie, and Ed Walsh that were published ten, twenty, or even thirty years after the fact. For decades, journalists and fans would track down participants in the battles of 1908 and ask them the same questions about the same events. In a classic series of interviews of old ballplayers conducted by Lawrence Ritter in the 1950s and 1960s and published under the title

The Glory of Their Times, the subject of 1908 comes up again and again.

The AL race was the closest in baseball history and, barring a major rules change, the closest there will ever be. The reason for this is that in 1908 teams contending for a pennant did not have to make up rain-outs or other postponements, even if they might affect the standings. Thus, in 1908, Detroit successfully defended its AL championship with a record of 90–63 in 153 games, one half game better than Cleveland, who played one more game and went 90–64. Today, Detroit would have to make up the extra game; if they lost, the pennant would be determined by a special playoff. Third-place Chicago played two fewer games in 1908, going 88–64, and thus might have made it a three-way tie if the full 154-game schedule had been completed.

For much of the 1908 AL season the St. Louis Browns were also in the hunt, led by strikeout king Rube Waddell, who was the era's poster boy for the stereotypical nuttiness of baseball left-handers. Philadelphia Athletics manager Connie Mack had sold Waddell in the off-season for $5,000 after tiring of his heavy drinking, habitual lateness, and childish passions for such things as hunting dogs and fire engines. In spite of the presence of Ty Cobb, Honus Wagner, and Larry Lajoie, the key figures in the race were all pitchers. The 1908 season culminated in an amazing series of pitching duels. Ed Walsh, Chicago's iron man spitballer, pitched a dozen shutouts and started seven of the White Sox' final nine games. On October 2, Walsh lost to Cleveland's Addie Joss, 1-0; Walsh struck out 15 batters but Joss picked that day to throw the major leagues' first perfect game since Cy Young in 1904. An undaunted Walsh beat Cleveland the following day and Detroit two days after that. When Big Bill Dineen of the Browns—who had faded from the race after Waddell announced that manager Jimmy McAleer knew "as much about baseball as a hog knows about skating" and walked out on the team—defeated Cleveland on the second to last day of the season, the Tigers held a slim half-game lead over both Cleveland and Chicago. The next afternoon Ty Cobb and the Tigers hitters finally reached the White Sox' Doc White and Ed Walsh for seven runs while Wild Bill Donovan threw a shutout to clinch the pennant. Cleveland beat St. Louis to finish a half-game out of first and one game ahead of third-place Chicago.

In 1908 it seemed as though every club had at least one pitcher who won 20 games with a sub-2.00 ERA. In the AL, Detroit's Ed Summers won 24 games with an ERA of 1.64; Boston's Cy Young won 21 games with an ERA of 1.26; and St. Louis's Harry Howell won 18 with an ERA of 1.89. Amazingly enough, however, none of these pitchers led the league in wins or ERA; Chicago workhorse Ed Walsh won 40 games and the brilliant Addie Joss of Cleveland pitched 325 innings with a minuscule ERA of 1.16!

THE YEAR: 1908

Nineteen-hundred-and-eight was the biggest year for pitching in a decade of pitchers' years. Both leagues batted .239, a record low. Seven pitchers threw no-hitters and seven of the fifty all-time lowest seasonal ERAs came in 1908; only one major league pitching staff, that of the New York Yankees, recorded an ERA over 3.00.

This wealth of pitching produced two of the closest, most exciting, and most controversial pennant races of all time. In the NL the 1908 Cubs exhibited their usual combination of overpowering pitching and slick defense, and Christy Mathewson, who led the league in wins, games, complete games, strikeouts, and ERA, carried the Giants. He threw a league-high 12 shutouts and recorded five saves (awarded retroactively by modern statisticians) pitching in a dozen games out of the bullpen between starts. The Giants made headlines in July by paying $11,000 for minor-league phenom pitcher Richard "Rube" Marquard. (Unlike most players called Rube, Marquard was not a country boy; he got his nickname because of his resemblence to Rube Waddell.) Once again, Pittsburgh was the Honus Wagner Show, as Wagner hit .354 and led the NL in on-base average at .410 and slugging average at .542. He also made a clean sweep of six other key offensive categories: hits, RBIs, doubles, triples, total bases, and stolen bases.

In the AL, a four-team race came down to the wire, with Detroit finally slipping past Cleveland by .004 in percentage points. Chicago finished 1½ back, and St. Louis faded late to end up 6½ behind. As in 1907, Cobb and Crawford led the AL in nearly everything. The AL's answer to Honus Wagner, Cobb won the batting title at .324 and was number one in hits, doubles, triples, total bases, RBIs, and slugging; Crawford led in home runs and was second in runs, RBIs, hits, total bases, batting, and slugging.

For the second straight year Cobb's team was humiliated in the World Series, this time 4–1. Cobb lived down his poor 1907 series performance by batting .368 with four RBIs and a pair of stolen bases. Cubs batters, however, hit .293 off Detroit pitching and Three Finger Brown's immaculate 0.00 ERA in 11 innings paced a Chicago staff that compiled a 2.60 ERA.

Nineteen-hundred-and-eight saw the publication of the song "Take Me Out to the Ball Game" by vaudevillian Jack Norworth. Legend has it that he wrote the lyrics while riding a Manhattan subway car full of fans on their way to the Polo Grounds. A confirmed non-baseball fan, Norworth actually attended his first baseball game as a guest of the Brooklyn Dodgers in 1942.

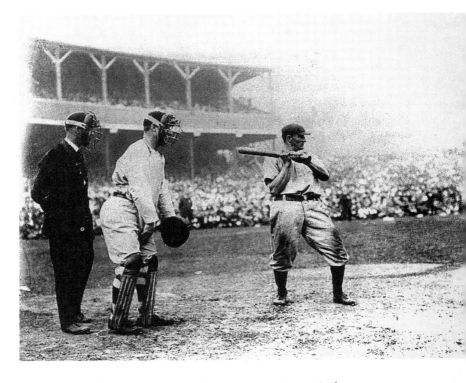

Pirates shortstop Honus Wagner awaits a pitch.
In 1908, Wagner hit .354 and led the NL in hits,
RBIs, doubles, triples, total bases, on-base average,
slugging average, and stolen bases.

On April 20, 1908, baseball lost Henry Chadwick, the English-born writer and editor whose early efforts in the promotion and development of baseball as a professional sport earned him the title The Father of Baseball. Chadwick contracted a fatal case of pneumonia after insisting on attending the Brooklyn Dodgers' home opener at Washington Park. At 83, Chadwick was still editing the prestigious *Spalding Guide* series of baseball annuals, as he had since 1881. Buried in Brooklyn's elegant Green-Wood cemetery, Chadwick remains the only writer to be enshrined not in the sportswriters' wing but in the main hall of the Hall of Fame in Cooperstown, beside the game's founding fathers and greatest stars.

The NL race of 1908 is better remembered today than its AL counterpart, despite having been a little less of a cliffhanger. There are two reasons for this. One is that the NL pennant turned on a single event, the Merkle blunder, that outdid anything that the AL race could offer for drama, pathos, and all-around zaniness. The other is that the NL pennant race involved a New York team and the history of baseball, the 1900s and 1910s included, has always been written more or less from a New York perspective.

For most of the summer of 1908, the NL pennant race was like a deadlocked heavyweight bout between skilled, determined fighters who give and take tremendous amounts of punishment without going down— except that in this case there were three men in the ring. Fred Clarke's Pittsburgh Pirates had won 93 games in 1906 and 91 in 1907 with little to show for it. Powering the Pirates was shortstop Honus Wagner, who would go on in 1908 to win the sixth of his eight career batting titles, and a deep pitching staff of Vic Willis, Howie Camnitz, Sam Leever, and Deacon Phillippe. But the hungry Pirates had not finished any closer than 17 games out of first place in either year, thanks to John McGraw's New York Giants and Frank Chance's Chicago Cubs. The Cubs made sure that there was no race in 1906 by winning 116 games, 20 more than the Giants, who narrowly beat out Pittsburgh for second place. In 1907 Chicago defended their championship with ease, winning 107 games.

No less hungry were the Giants, whose magnificent pitching staff of Christy Mathewson, Joe McGinnity,

Red Ames, and George "Hooks" Wiltse had been out-classed in both races by the Cubs' murderers' row of Brown, Reulbach, Pfiester, Overall, and Lundgren. In 1908, however, Chicago was not able to get away from the pack. On September 21, New York's record stood at 87–47, 3½ games ahead of the Cubs and 4 up on the Pirates, thanks to Mathewson's heroic pitching and the splendid hitting of Turkey Mike Donlin. One of manager McGraw's more successful reclamation projects, Donlin was an erratic drunk and dandy with a weakness for show business—and actresses. Before retiring in 1914 to go on the vaudeville stage, Donlin gave McGraw two good seasons; one of them was 1908, when he batted .356 and led the NL in runs scored with 124. In late September the race began to tighten up. The Pirates beat New York on September 22; on the following day the Cubs came to New York and swept a doubleheader in which shortstop Al Bridwell came to bat numerous times with men in scoring position and two outs and failed to get a hit.

The Cubs and Giants met again on the 23rd of September. This was the contest that has gone down in history as the single strangest, messiest, most famous game of the entire dead-ball era. It began calmly enough. After Mathewson and Pfiester had dueled for 8½ innings, the score stood at 1-1. With two outs in the bottom of the ninth the Giants had a chance to win the game; Bridwell stepped up to the plate with outfielder Harry "Moose" McCormick on third and Fred Merkle on first. Merkle, a 19-year-old rookie first baseman, had pinch-hit for the injured regular, Fred Tenney. A tense Polo Grounds crowd rooted for Bridwell to redeem himself for the previous day and come through in the clutch. He responded with a clean single to center field, apparently winning the game, and sent several thousand Giants fans spilling onto the field and on their happy way home.

Few fans took any notice of the bizarre scene that was unfolding on the field after the game's final play; most went home, had dinner, and enjoyed a good night's sleep before reading in the next morning's paper that their team had not, in fact, won the game, 2-1. What happened? Nearly everyone who was there that day offered a slightly different account. The Cubs' version is that instead of running 90 feet and touching second base, Fred Merkle saw the crowd swarming onto the infield and headed straight for the Giants' clubhouse, which was located behind the center-field fence. Realizing that, according to a strict reading of the rules, if Merkle were forced at second for the third out of the inning, McCormick's run would not count, Johnny Evers called for center fielder Artie Hofman to throw him the ball at second base. Giants pitcher Joe McGinnity saw what was happening, intercepted the throw, and heaved it either into or over the grandstand. The Cubs claimed that they then retrieved that same ball and tagged second base while field umpire Bob Emslie and plate umpire Hank O'Day were physically prevented from leaving the field by Frank Chance and several teammates. The umpires later said that they had declared Merkle out but did not offer any reason why they had not attempted to clear the field and resume the game, which presumably would have been tied, 1-1, going into the top of the tenth. The *New York Sun* reported that O'Day conferred with his partner and then mumbled: "Emslie says he didn't see the play at second base, and it's no game I suppose."

After the game, confusion reigned. In a locker room interview O'Day told the *New York Herald* that he had seen Merkle fail to touch second and that he had therefore ruled the game a tie. McGinnity admitted grabbing the ball and throwing it into the grandstand but accused the Cubs of fishing another ball out of a ball bag and substituting it for the game ball. Merkle swore that he had gone back and touched second base while McGinnity and several Cubs players were wrestling over the ball. He was backed up by that paragon of sportsmanship, Christy Mathewson, as well as the *New York Evening Mail,* which reported that "Merkle got to second. He started late, but he got there. The ball never did."[1] Manager McGraw said that "the game had been won fairly" and added: "How can the umpires decide it is no game? Umpires can't go out on the field and make rules. Either the game should be declared forfeited on account of the crowd overrunning the field . . . or it was won by us. . . . The play in the ninth inning wasn't a question of interpretation of the rules, which is the only ground on which protest can be made."[2] Under the rules of the time, McGraw was perfectly correct.

The next day, however, NL president Harry Pulliam answered none of McGraw's points. He announced only that he was backing his umpires; the game was officially a tie and would be replayed, if necessary, after the season. This was what is now known as a cop-out; Pulliam was trying to defuse the controversy and hoping against hope that the replay would not be necessary. Pulliam's decision, however, only added more fuel to the bitter nationwide debate over the "Merkle blunder," as the incident was becoming known. Chicago sportswriters and fans applauded Pulliam and the umpires. "Rules are rules, and clubs having boneheaded mutts on the base paths deserve only to be penalized. All honor to Hank O'Day," wrote the *Chicago Journal,* "There has been much roasting of Hank . . . on account of the exactly similar Pittsburgh affair some weeks ago. . . . But Hank has shown the genuine goods, and has put himself on record as an honest umpire and a good man."[3]

The so-called "Pittsburgh affair" was a game that had taken place between the Pirates and Cubs on September 4, where an eerily similar scenario had played out. With two outs in the bottom of the tenth and the bases loaded with Pirates, Pittsburgh outfielder Owen Wilson singled up the middle to score Fred Clarke from third. Noticing that rookie first baseman Warren Gill, the base runner on first, had sprinted off the field without touching second, Evers called for the ball and tagged second base. The game ended anyway, however, because umpire Hank O'Day, working the game solo (most NL games in the 1900s used only a single umpire), was not having any of it. "Clarke was over the plate," he said, "so his run counted anyway." Technically speaking, of course, the timing of Clarke's run should have been irrelevant if the third out was made on a force play. Over the next few days O'Day was stung by criticism of his call in the Pittsburgh game from Cubs president Charles Murphy and others; this undoubtedly put him in a frame of mind to pay extra attention to similar plays in the future.

New York fans and writers were outraged. Setting aside McGraw's very valid points about the illogic of declaring the game a tie, the argument over the Merkle blunder boiled down, like the modern Pine Tar game controversy, to a question of the letter versus the spirit of the rules. In many ways, the Merkle affair resembled the Pine Tar incident of 1983, in which a home run by George Brett of the Kansas City Royals was nullified after Yankees manager Billy Martin pointed out that Brett's bat had an illegal amount of pine tar on the barrel. AL president Lee MacPhail later reversed the umpire's decision. The *New York Herald* summed up the issues in the Merkle affair perfectly:

> *In fact, all our boys did rather well if Fred Merkle could gather the idea into his noodle that baseball custom does not permit a runner to take a shower and some light lunch in the clubhouse on the way to second. Then again, taking*

*it on the whole, an enormous baseball custom
has had it from time immemorial that as soon as
the winning run has crossed the plate everyone
adjourns as hastily and yet nicely as possible to
the clubhouse and exits.*[4]

If Hank O'Day was hoping to avoid public criticism by
his handling of the Merkle blunder, he was sorely disappointed. Respected fellow umpire Bill Klem called it
the worst baseball decision he had ever heard of. NL
president Pulliam was widely ridiculed, especially in
New York City, where he lived and worked. Prominent
sportswriter Sam Crane of the *New York Evening-Journal,*
who had played big-league baseball back in the 1880s,
wrote, "I have never seen local lovers of the game so
fairly boiling over with anger as they were yesterday
when President Pulliam's decision was announced."

No one, however, suffered more conspicuously
than young Merkle. By the last few days of the season,
Christy Mathewson writes in his book *Pitching in a
Pinch,* "Merkle had lost twenty pounds, and his eyes
were hollow and his cheeks sunken. The newspapers
showed him no mercy, and the fans never failed to criti-
cize and hiss him when he appeared on the field." He
became known as Bonehead Merkle, a nickname that
stuck with him for the rest of his 16 years in the majors.
Wherever he went on or off the field, there was always
a wise guy to say, "So long, Fred, and don't forget to
touch second." *Touching Second,* by the way, was the
name chosen by Johnny Evers for the baseball book that
he co-wrote with sportswriter Hugh Fullerton in 1910.

Fate was not through with Fred Merkle or, for that
matter, Harry Pulliam. Partly thanks to Phillies pitcher
Harry "The Giant Killer" Coveleski, who defeated the
Giants three times in less than a week immediately after
the Merkle game, the Cubs and Giants finished the
1908 season with identical records of 98–55. Pulliam's

worst nightmare had come true. The teams met on October 8 to replay the September 23rd game; to the winner would go the NL flag. Mathewson and Pfiester were the starters, but when a wild Pfiester was removed by Frank Chance after allowing a run in the first inning, Three Finger Brown took over for Chicago. Brown and Mathewson had squared off in dozens of big games over the years, but none was bigger than this one. In the third, Joe Tinker, who always gave Mathewson trouble, led off with a ringing triple that kicked off a four-run rally. Brown gave up only a single run and Chicago won the game 4-2.

The 1908 season may have come to an end, but the controversy over the Merkle blunder raged on. Manager John McGraw, who was known for his intolerance of what he termed "mental errors" and who could brow-beat and humiliate a player with the best of them, stood squarely in Merkle's corner. He defended Merkle publicly every chance he got, made him the regular first baseman in 1910, and put his name in the Giants line-up nearly every day for the next seven years. But he was still Bonehead Merkle to the fans, and they never let him forget it. In a 1915 interview, a reporter asked Merkle if he had fun playing baseball.

"No," Merkle answered, "I wouldn't call it fun. I have too rough a time out there."

"Do the fans still ride you?"

"Yes. The worst thing is I can't do things other players do without attracting attention. Little slips that would be excused in other players are burned into me by the crowds. . . . If any play I'm concerned with goes wrong, I'm the fellow who gets the blame, no matter where the thing went off the line."

The passage of time did little to diminish Merkle's stature as a famous goat.

Historian Lee Allen told of running into an aged Fred Merkle in a Florida bar during the 1950s; Merkle took one look at Allen and said: "You want to know about the play, I guess."[5]

As for NL president Pulliam, he became increasingly distracted. A bachelor with a fussy, nervous temperament who was extremely sensitive to public criticism, Pulliam was going through a personal hell during the off-season of 1908–09. Disturbed by the erratic, almost paranoid, tone of some of his public statements, the baseball owners urged Pulliam to take a leave of absence, after which he appeared to be fully recovered and resumed his duties. On the evening of July 28, 1909, however, Pulliam closed the door of his home, an apartment at the New York Athletic Club, changed into his night clothes, loaded a pistol, and shot himself in the head. He died the next morning. No one will ever know how much the Merkle affair contributed, if at all, to Pulliam's mental problems or his death; it is known that he was increasingly troubled by the political intriguing and back stabbing of his employers, the baseball owners. But it could not have helped. If the story of the 1908 NL pennant race means anything, it may be that as major-league baseball became more competitive, attracted more fans, and became an ever bigger business in the dead-ball era, it began to take itself more and more seriously. As Fred Merkle and Harry Pulliam could tell you, this had a down side.

CHAPTER FIVE

Against the Grain: Honus Wagner and Ty Cobb

Baseball in the dead-ball era was dominated in every way by pitchers. The poor, unfortunate hitters of the time fought a two-decade-long losing battle against the likes of Walter Johnson's and Rube Waddell's fastball, Jack Chesbro's and Ed Walsh's spitter, Cy Young's and Addie Joss's control, and Christy Mathewson's fadeaway—not to mention dirty, scuffed baseballs, huge strike zones, and cavernous ballparks with unreachable outfield fences.

Strangely enough, however, the dead-ball era also produced two of the greatest hitters ever to have played the game, two men who put up 1890s-like numbers in spite of batting in lineups full of .230-hitting third basemen and .198-hitting catchers. One of them, shortstop Honus Wagner of the Pittsburgh Pirates, batted .329 lifetime over 21 National League seasons. He won eight batting titles and hit .300 or better in a season a record 17 times. Even though many of his records have been surpassed by players from later eras when hits, runs, and home runs were easier to come by, Wagner remains among the top 10 hitters all-time in most major statistical categories. As recently as 1960, he still held the NL records for career games played, at-bats, hits, singles, and triples.

The other great hitter of the dead-ball era, outfielder Ty Cobb of the Detroit Tigers, played in the American League. Far inferior to Wagner as a defensive player, Cobb was a slightly better hitter. He batted an incredible .367 lifetime against dead-ball pitching, leading the league in batting 12 times. From 1907 to 1919, 13 seasons in which it has never been harder to get a hit or score a run in the major leagues, Cobb scored over 100 runs seven times, drove in more than 100 runs five times, and batted .350, .324, .377, .385, .420, .410, .390, .368, .369, .371, .383, .382, and .384.

For some reason, Ty Cobb is much better remembered by today's baseball fans than Honus Wagner. Part of the reason may be Cobb's fascinating personality; part of it may be the fact that Wagner was funny looking, with a physique—comically bowed legs, a barrel chest, huge hands, and a large nose—that gave no hint of his abundant speed, grace, and power. People who met him in his postplaying days, when he had put on weight, had trouble believing that he had ever been a great fielder or a champion base stealer. Like Yogi Berra, another great athlete with a comical appearance, Wagner became a convenient subject for all kinds of corny, and mostly phony, baseball folk tales, many of which portray him as some kind of clown. This has tended to obscure the memory of his greatness as a ballplayer. In any case, it was Wagner, not Cobb, whom contemporary baseball authorities like Branch Rickey, John McGraw, and Ed Barrow rated as the greatest all-around baseball player ever. All three of these men had seen Babe Ruth play; Barrow was the manager who changed the course of baseball history by deciding to play Ruth, then a pitcher with the Boston Red Sox, every day in the outfield and see how many home runs he could hit. In Barrow's words,

> *Babe Ruth was the game's greatest personality, and its greatest home run hitter. Ty Cobb was the greatest of the hitters, and the only man I ever saw who could unnerve a whole ball club single-handed, though I have always had a tremendous admiration for Larry Lajoie and consider him only a step behind Cobb as the greatest batsman of them all. But there is no question that Wagner was the greatest all-around ballplayer who ever lived.*[1]

In fact it was Barrow who discovered Honus Wagner and later insisted that he could play shortstop. In his 1951 memoir, *My Fifty Years in Baseball,* Barrow tells the story of how he traveled to the coal-mining country of western Pennsylvania and found the 21-year-old German immigrant's son, whose nickname Honus (pronounced "Honn'-iss", not "Hoe'-niss") was short for the German name Johannes, tossing rocks along the railroad tracks. "He threw with a great sweep and no effort," Barrow writes, "and as I watched the rocks sail a couple of hundred feet up the track I knew I had to have this fellow on my ball club." Barrow actually rediscovered Wagner; he had played one season in the low minors before quitting because of homesickness. Wagner signed to play for Barrow's Paterson, New Jersey, club in the minor Atlantic League, where he hit .348. The following year he landed in the majors when Barrow sold him to the NL club in Louisville, Kentucky. He hit .344, .305, and .359 for Louisville from 1897 to 1899, when the club was dropped by the NL and its owner, Barney Dreyfuss, transferred its best players to his other NL club, the Pittsburgh Pirates.

From 1900 until the end of his career in 1917, Honus Wagner was the heart and soul of the Pirates, leading the team to four pennants and three world championships. Wagner's glorious career is even more impressive when you consider that he got a late start in pro ball and that he was used as a utility man by manager Fred Clarke until 1903, when at the urging of Ed Barrow he was finally given the starting shortstop job for good at the age of 29. Many of Wagner's awesome career numbers were piled up late in his baseball life. He won a batting title at 37, stole 23 bases at 40, hit 17 triples at 41, and played 92 games at shortstop when he was 42. When his playing days were over, he remained with Pittsburgh for many years as a coach. After his retirement, a bronze statue of the beloved Wagner was set up outside Pittsburgh's Forbes Field. Today the statue has been relocated to the Pirates' current home, Three Rivers Stadium, near the statue of modern Pirates great Roberto Clemente.

Part of the Honus Wagner legend was his unassuming, humble, and honest character in a cynical and increasingly corrupt era in baseball. Wagner was known to dislike haggling over money and was underpaid for most of his career. He passed up many opportunities to add to his income by appearing in vaudeville shows or barnstorming tours; Wagner was one of the few major NL stars to refuse a huge raise in pay to jump to the AL in 1901 and 1902. In 1910, he turned down a salesman for a tobacco company that wanted to print Honus Wagner baseball cards as a promotion for its products. It was a moral issue for Wagner; even though he chewed tobacco and smoked cigars, he did not approve of tobacco advertising on the grounds that smoking was bad for the health of young people. Characteristically, however, Wagner sent the salesman a check for the $10 commission he would have received

Honus Wagner's portrait appears on this early baseball card. Many baseball experts consider Wagner the best all-around baseball player ever.

for getting Wagner's permission to use his picture. Unfortunately, the company had already begun distributing the cards, so it had to recall and destroy as many of them as possible. Today there are no more than a dozen in existence, and the 1910 Honus Wagner card is the Holy Grail of baseball collectibles. One sold recently for a price rumored to have been between $500,000 and $1 million.

A clubhouse leader who was revered by teammates and known for his kindness to young players—dead-ball-era rookies were more typically subjected to brutal hazing by big-league veterans—Honus Wagner possessed a rare blend of toughness and gentleness. His popularity with fans, even fans of other teams, was remarkable; according to historian and Cincinnati native Lee Allen, "[Wagner] was probably cheered more on the road than any other player in history, and his popularity reached the stage of adulation in Cincinnati, where Germans . . . cheered to the rafters his every move."

Sometimes, Wagner's gentle side was misinterpreted by opponents as weakness. During the 1909 World Series between Pittsburgh and Detroit, which was hyped as a personal battle between baseball's two biggest superstars, Honus Wagner and Ty Cobb faced each other for the first time. After reaching first base in the second game, Cobb shouted in the direction of the Pirates shortstop: "Hey krauthead! I'm coming down on the next pitch." Cobb was not giving away much by telegraphing his stolen base attempt. The meanest, most aggressive base runner ever, Cobb owed his base running success more to intimidation than to speed or surprise. Whether or not the rumors were true that he sharpened the metal spikes on his baseball shoes, he used them to slice up many a middle infielder's shins. Honus Wagner, however, was not afraid. "I'll be waiting," he called back to Cobb. When, seconds later, Cobb did come flying into second base with his spikes in the air, Wagner calmly fielded the throw from catcher George Gibson and swipe-tagged Cobb in the teeth. Cobb never recovered; when the series was over, he had a split lip and only two stolen bases to Wagner's six. The Pirates won the world championship, four games to three.

THE YEAR: 1909

The 1909 Cubs won 104 games, normally more than enough to win the pennant, but this time Honus Wagner and the resurgent Pirates finally put it all together, going 110–42 and taking the NL flag by 6½ games. Wagner was the engine that drove the Pittsburgh offense to a league-best 699 runs scored; he won his seventh batting title, hitting .339, and banged out 39 doubles and 100 RBIs. The secret to playing with Honus Wagner was to get on base any way you could and wait for him to drive you in. Manager-outfielder Fred Clarke led the NL with 80 walks and third baseman Bobby Byrne was second with 78. Outfielder Tommy Leach scored 126 runs, second-most in the league; Clarke 97, third-most; and Bobby Byrne 92, fourth-most. Thanks to their dominant hitting and a much-improved Pittsburgh pitching staff that included Howie Camnitz, who went 25–6, and 22-game winner Vic Willis, the Pirates led from May 5 until the final day of the season.

The New York Giants won 92 games to finish third. Christy Mathewson led the NL in ERA at 1.14, the fourth-best seasonal mark ever. Larry Doyle's league-leading 172 hits and John "Red" Murray's 91 RBIs paced the Giants offense.

In the AL it was a two-team battle between Detroit, the defending champion and winner the previous two seasons, and Connie Mack's maturing Philadelphia dynasty. The A's infield featured 23-year-old Frank

The 1909 Boston Red Sox at their spring training camp in Hot Springs, Arkansas

"Home Run" Baker and 22-year-olds Jack Barry and Eddie Collins, three-quarters of what would become Philadelphia's famed $100,000 Infield. The pitching staff was anchored by Harry Krause, whose 1.39 ERA nosed out Ed Walsh's 1.41 for the ERA title. Third baseman Baker and outfielder Danny Murphy combined for 33 triples and supplied the power for a late-season charge that carried the A's briefly past Detroit. Ty Cobb enjoyed the best season of his career and dominated the AL at least as much as Wagner did the NL. He led the league in batting and slugging; he was also first in the AL in runs with 116, RBIs with 107, stolen bases with 76, and on-base average at .431.

Cleveland shortstop Neal Ball made history in a July 19, 1909, game against Boston when he turned the 20th century's first unassisted triple play.

The 1909 season saw the first two modern steel-and-concrete ballparks, Shibe Park in Philadelphia and Forbes Field in Pittsburgh, open for business. Another first was the first-ever seven-game World Series, won by Pittsburgh. While the fans who came to see a Cobb-Wagner match-up were disappointed—Wagner had a good series, hitting .333, but Cobb flopped completely, batting .231—the series was a thrilling, closely fought contest in which the teams alternated victories throughout. The series hero was 27-year-old rookie Charles "Babe" Adams, who had gone 12–3 during the season with a 1.11 ERA in a spot-starting role. Adams's junk held the great Cobb to a single hit in 11 at-bats as he won games one, five, and seven to finish 3–0 with a 1.33 ERA for the series. This was the last postseason appearance for Detroit until 1935 and the last time ever that Cobb and Wagner played on the same field.

Ty Cobb may have failed to intimidate Honus Wagner, but after becoming a regular outfielder with Detroit in 1907, Cobb had managed to intimidate the rest of the American League. The positive side of Cobb was that he produced on the field. In spite of occasional brief periods when he would seem to slip into an emotional funk or nurse a minor injury, he put up offensive numbers that surpass those of any other dead-ball hitter. In 1908 he hit a league-leading 20 triples and won his second batting title; in 1909 he batted .377 and stole 76 bases and, according to Lee Allen, "replaced Rube Waddell as the biggest drawing card in the game." For the 10 years after that, Cobb topped the AL in so many offensive categories that it would be easier to list the ones he did not lead in. He regularly hit over 40 doubles, over 20 triples, scored over 100 runs, recorded over

The mighty Cobb awaits his turn at bat. When he retired in 1928, Ty Cobb had established records for career batting average (.367), hits (4,191), runs scored (2,245), stolen bases (892), and batting titles (12).

200 hits, and stole over 60 bases. When his career came to an end at the age of 41, he had become the first and only man to play 3,000 AL games or collect 4,000 hits. Today, he remains number one all-time in batting average and runs scored. Only Lou Brock and Rickey Henderson have bettered his 892 career stolen bases.

Although Cobb is thought of today primarily as a singles or doubles hitter, he had real power—possibly even as much as Babe Ruth, had Cobb chosen to swing for the fences. In 1911, with a little help from the cork-centered baseball, Cobb would bat an amazing .420, score 147 runs, drive in 144, have a 40-game hit streak, and record a slugging average of .621. No AL hitter would equal Cobb's 1911 slugging mark until Babe Ruth slugged .657 in 1919. When the baseball rules were changed to encourage the long ball in the 1920s, Cobb refused to change his magic hitting stroke and continued to hit for singles, doubles, and batting average. In 1925, however, tired of all of the hoopla over Babe Ruth and the new generation of young home run hitters, Cobb told a group of skeptical reporters that hitting home runs was no great trick, all it took was moving the hands down to the knob of the bat and taking a big cut. He then went out and proved it: he hit five home runs in two days before going back to his normal line-drive swing.

Ty Cobb never had it easy in baseball; he owed most of his success not to outstanding speed or strength but to a burning, all-consuming competitiveness. When he was a teenager trying to make a minor-league club far from his Georgia home, his mother shot his father with a shotgun and stood trial for murder. Cobb's stern, emotionally distant father had disapproved of his son's choice of baseball as a career, but the last thing the elder Cobb said to him before his death was "Don't come home a failure." These words rang in Cobb's ears throughout his 30 years in professional baseball. He refused to fail, battling his way to the majors at 18 and standing up to the vicious treatment that rookies of the time were expected to take from veterans. Fearing that he might take the job of a popular teammate, Cobb's fellow Tigers broke his bats, cut up his clothes, pushed him out of the batting cage, and, on one occasion, physically assaulted him. Cobb's reaction was to fight back even harder. Remembering his rookie year in his 1961 autobiography, Cobb writes, "the attitude of my teammates gave me the extra incentive of becoming a top player in order to show them up."

Ty Cobb's angry determination, however, produced an undeniable dark side. He was tightly wound, with an intense, unpleasant demeanor, and a dangerous, hair-trigger temper. His 24-year career in the major leagues was punctuated by numerous unsavory and controversial incidents, many of them involving his obsessive hatred of African-Americans. He became the most unpopular visiting player of the decade in Philadelphia when his spikes sliced a gash in the arm of Athletics third baseman and fan favorite Home Run Baker in August 1909. Cobb once assaulted an African-American construction worker in Detroit because he resented the man telling him to stay off a stretch of wet asphalt; after an argument over a cut of meat at a Detroit butcher shop, Cobb spent a night in jail for pistol-whipping the butcher's African-American assistant. Southerners were rare in dead-ball-era baseball, and a favorite theme of northern hecklers and bench jockeys was to suggest that Cobb and other southern players had African-American ancestry. As Cobb later described one insult that provoked him to challenge teammate Ed Siever to a fistfight, "Where I came from, men had been killed for saying [that]."

Racial heckling led to one of the blackest marks on Cobb's career. Playing in New York's Hilltop Park in 1912, Cobb was being ridden verbally by a Yankee fan named Claude Lueker. In the third inning, when Lueker called the Tigers outfielder a "half-nigger," Cobb leaped into the stands like a wild animal and, in the words of the victim, "hit me in the face with his fist, knocked me down, jumped on me, kicked me, spiked me, and booted me behind the ear." Cobb's reaction to Lueker's statement showed no trace of remorse: "I'm pleased to note," he writes, "that I didn't overlook any important punitive measures." What Cobb does not mention in his own account of the incident is that Lueker was handicapped; he was missing one entire hand and three fingers on the other. The incident caused a public uproar. It should be noted, however, that even the New York media criticized Cobb for attacking a disabled person, not for reacting violently to a racial insult; most sportswriters seem to have felt that any gentleman would have behaved the same way.

AL president Ban Johnson suspended Cobb indefinitely for the Hilltop Park attack; this led to baseball's first player strike. When the rest of the Tigers protested by refusing to play their next game against the Athletics, Detroit manager Hughie Jennings was forced to field a pickup team of coaches and amateurs pulled off the street in order to avoid a forfeit and a fine. With 48-year-old ex–major leaguer Deacon McGuire behind the plate and young seminary student Aloysius Travers on the mound, the "paper" Tigers lost to Philadelphia by a score of 24-2. The embarrassment caused by this game led Johnson to settle the strike the next day by agreeing to reinstate Cobb after 10 days.

As great as he was with the bat and on the base paths, Cobb was a no better than above-average outfielder with a weak arm and a bitter, corrosive personality. Besides being an unabashed racist, Ty Cobb was violent, uncouth, and so disliked by his peers that they conspired to take a batting title away from him by giving rival Larry Lajoie eight gift hits in a doubleheader on the final day of the 1910 season. Some psychologists have speculated that Ty Cobb may have been, at times, psychotic. The best-fielding shortstop of the dead-ball era, Wagner was a greater all-around player and a generous, positive presence in the clubhouse. The complete record of fights, scandals, and controversies involving Wagner would be a blank book. The modern writer who described Honus Wagner as a combination of "the speed and daring of Rickey Henderson, the arm of Roberto Clemente, the bat of Ty Cobb, the power of Babe Ruth, the glove of Ozzie Smith, and the character of Lou Gehrig."[2] exaggerated only a little. As different as they were in character, however, as baseball players Wagner and Cobb had a great deal in common. Both were awesome offensive forces that went against the grain of the times in which they played. With the odds stacked against them, both put up numbers that compare with those of Babe Ruth, Mickey Mantle, Frank Thomas, Barry Bonds, and the other superstars of more hitter-friendly eras.

C H A P T E R
S I X

"*I*t's Great to Be Young and a Giant!": Dead-ball Dynasties

The dead-ball era was a time of baseball dynasties, dominated by New York and Chicago in the NL, and Philadelphia and Boston in the AL. Among them, these four franchises won 23 of the 38 pennants contested by the 16 major-league clubs between 1901 and 1919. At the other end of the scale were four teams that failed to win a single pennant in the dead-ball decades—the Yankees, Senators, and both St. Louis clubs—and four teams that won one pennant each—the Boston Braves, the Phillies, the Reds, and the Cleveland Indians. If you look at it another way, success in the dead-ball era was even less evenly distributed than that: twelve pennants, about one-third of the total, were won by only two men, former 1890s stars John McGraw and Connie Mack. Sons of Irish immigrants, like so many other NL players of the 1890s, McGraw and Mack were the great baseball minds who designed, built, and ran the New York Giants and the Philadelphia Athletics.

When the 30-year-old John McGraw took over the New York Giants in the middle of the 1902 season, he had his work cut out. Thanks to the mismanagement of owner Andrew Freedman, the franchise was a disaster area. Freedman had hired and fired 13 managers in eight years—two in the first three months of 1902 alone. It had been 13 years since the team had won an NL pennant and five years since it had finished in the first division. McGraw, however, had two things going for him that Freedman's other managers had not. One was that he had a long-term plan for how to rebuild the team. The other was that he had been guaranteed the time to make his plan work; when he came over from the AL, he had insisted on a four-year contract that gave him "absolute control" over all baseball decisions.

Over Freedman's protests, McGraw cleared out the Giants' dead wood by releasing most of the team's highly paid veterans and replacing them with Dan McGann, Roger Bresnahan, Joe McGinnity, and other players stolen from his former club, the AL Baltimore Orioles. He also undid some of the work of his predecessors, Horace Fogel and Heinie Smith, by moving the 22-year-old Christy Mathewson from first base back into the pitching rotation. It was too late for any of McGraw's moves to save the 1902 season—the team finished a franchise-record 53½ games behind Fred Clarke's Pittsburgh Pirates—but 1903 would be a different story.

In 1903 the Giants were bought by former Reds owner John Brush, Ban Johnson's old enemy. This was fine with McGraw, who was Johnson's second-least-favorite person; Brush was a hands-off owner who was content to give McGraw free rein as long as things went well. Starting with McGraw's first full year in charge of the team, things began to go very, very well. The New York Giants soon became the greatest of the dead-ball dynasties, contending or winning the pennant nearly every year. The Giants came in second in 1903 and went on to finish first or second in 12 out of the next 16 years.

After they won back-to-back NL pennants in 1904 and 1905, beating Connie Mack's Philadelphia Athletics handily to win the second modern World Series, McGraw and his team became the toast of the town. The Giants filled the Polo Grounds, drawing 910,000 fans in 1908 and nearly five million for the decade; both figures led the majors. Nicknamed The Little Napoleon for his tactical brilliance, McGraw became a special favorite of the Broadway set. Actors George M. Cohan and DeWolfe Hopper (the man who made "Casey at the Bat" famous) were regular fixtures in the field boxes at Giants games; and less wholesome types, such as underworld fixer Arnold Rothstein and other organized crime figures, socialized with McGraw at the ballpark or at McGraw's palatial Herald Square pool hall. At a civic banquet thrown for the team in 1907, rookie second baseman Larry Doyle exclaimed: "It's great to be young and a Giant!" Teams inside and outside of organized baseball sought to borrow some of the New York club's glory by adopting the name Giants; among the top African-American clubs of the dead-ball era, for instance, there were the Cuban Giants, the Cuban Ex-Giants, the Royal Giants, the Philadelphia Giants, and others.

The basis of John McGraw's success was threefold. First, he had an unerring eye for baseball talent and was decisive about personnel decisions. Second, he enforced a Ned Hanlon–style program of team discipline, conducting daily morning workouts to keep players' skills sharp and to discourage late nights. Starting in 1908, McGraw became the first major-league manager to establish a permanent spring training camp with its own facilities. He located the Giants' camp in the remote backwater of Marlin, Texas, an alcohol-free town with little night life beyond the occasional fish fry and nothing for his normally hard-partying players to do but work. There the team took daily jogs along the railroad

The New York Giants' John McGraw, nicknamed The Little Napoleon because of his authoritarian managerial style, was respected as a brilliant strategist and a keen judge of talent.

tracks in the hot Texas sun, practiced sliding in sand pits that McGraw had invented for that purpose, and worked on the hit-and-run and other dead-ball fundamentals.

Finally, McGraw was unmatched as a game manager, refining the techniques of all-out aggression and psychological intimidation that he had learned in his Orioles days. His philosophy is best described by his famous statement: "The main idea is to win." To that end he would do anything, legal or illegal, that he thought he could get away with. McGraw pioneered the use of platooning, or sharing positions between a right-handed and left-handed hitter. He was a master of verbal and psychological abuse of umpires and of his own or opposing players. Sportswriters often remarked on McGraw's "Jekyll and Hyde" personality; he could be incredibly vile to an umpire or to a Giants player who made a "mental mistake," but he could also be kind, loyal, and generous, as in the case of Fred Merkle or Fred Snodgrass. McGraw's behavior toward pitcher Arthur "Bugs" Raymond is typical. One of many alcoholics that McGraw tried to rescue during his managerial career, Raymond was a hopeless case who died at 30 in a drunken brawl. McGraw tried everything to save the young pitcher, including fining him a total of $1,700 out of his $4,200 salary in 1909. Raymond never found out that McGraw was secretly sending the money to Raymond's wife and children.

While his iron discipline and domineering style could rankle veteran players, McGraw was revered by the younger generation of Giants who came along in the middle 1900s. "What a great man he was!" remembered pitcher Rube Marquard, "The finest and grandest man I ever met. Of course he wouldn't stand for any nonsense. . . . When he laid down the law you'd better abide by it." Perhaps because of his own experiences with anti-Irish discrimination in the 19th century, McGraw was especially sympathetic to African-American and Native American players. He signed catcher Chief Meyers and Olympic champion Jim Thorpe, both Native Americans, and never stopped trying to sneak African-American stars past baseball's color line. In 1901 he almost convinced the baseball world that the African-American second baseman Charlie Grant was a Cherokee Indian named Chief Tokahoma. On another occasion he plotted to tutor a couple of African-American players in Spanish, send them to Havana, and then have them immigrate to the United States as Cubans. After his death in 1934, McGraw's wife revealed that her husband kept a running list of top African-American prospects, in case baseball ever decided to re-integrate.

THE YEAR: 1910

The 1910 season ushered in yet another decade of dead ball. As it had been since the advent of the foul-strike rule, baseball for most of the 1910s was a low-scoring affair that depended heavily on pitching, defense, and the running game. The NL compiled league ERAs under 3.00 in six seasons, the AL in seven. Once again, the greatest stars were pitchers, and late in the decade a new generation arrived to take over from Mathewson, Young, and Brown. Like those of their predecessors, the names of Walter Johnson and Pete Alexander still dot the pitching record books.

The 1910s also saw two trends that would ulti-mately contribute to the rise of modern home-run ori-ented baseball in the 1920s: the new phenomenon of enclosed steel-and-concrete ballparks and the adoption of the livelier cork-centered baseball. Three parks built in the 1910s—Boston's Fenway Park, Detroit's Tiger Stadium, and Chicago's Wrigley Field—are still in use today; the grandest was the White Sox' Comiskey Park, which was considered the finest baseball facility in the world when it opened in 1910 with a staggering capacity of 48,600. The cork-centered ball was invented by Philadelphia owner Ben Shibe; after a successful exper-iment with its use in the 1910 World Series, it was adopted by both leagues for the following season.

Already known as "the dean of managers"—who knew that he would manage the A's for another 41 years?—Connie Mack brought his team in at 102–48, 14½ games ahead of second-place New York. Philadelphia featured a veteran pitching staff of 31-game-winner Jack Coombs, Chief Bender, Harry "Cy" Morgan, and Eddie Plank, and a young lineup that included Eddie Collins, Jack Barry, and Frank Baker, all under 25 years of age. One of the greatest second basemen in history, Collins led the league in stolen bases with 81 and his team in RBIs with 81; he hit .322. Baker, Collins, and powerful outfielders Danny Murphy and Rube Oldring all reached double figures in triples. The A's ran away with the AL flag after beating back a midsummer challenge from Ty Cobb's Tigers. Cobb himself led the league in runs with 106, on-base average at .456, and slugging at .554; his only rival as a hitter was Cleveland's Lajoie, who appeared to have beat out Cobb for the batting title by a single point on the last day of the season.

The Cobb/Lajoie rivalry intensified after the Chalmers Motor Car Company, in a promotion that inspired the modern MVP award, offered an automobile to the winner of the 1910 AL batting title. The 1910 batting race ended in scandal when the St. Louis Browns lay back and gave Lajoie eight hits, including six bunt hits, on the last day of the season in order to deprive the hated Cobb of the batting title and a Chalmers "30" roadster. AL president Ban Johnson declared Cobb the real winner; the Browns' manager was fired for his part in the plot. To prevent future corruption, the Chalmers award was allowed to continue only on the basis that it be given to the "most important and useful" player in each league as determined by a committee of sportswriters, not to the leader in any statistical category.

Frank Chance's Chicago club went 104–50 to win its fourth NL pennant in five years. Outfielder Artie Hofman led the club in hitting at .325 and RBIs with 86, and

Larry Lajoie (left) and Ty Cobb pose in a Chalmers "30" roadster, the prize for winning the 1910 AL batting title. Because of the controversy surrounding that year's batting title, the Chalmers Motor Company awarded a car to both men.

Frank "Wildfire" Schulte led the league in home runs with 10. Rookie pitcher Leonard "King" Cole went 20–4 with a league-low 1.80 ERA and Three Finger Brown went 25–13 with the NL's second-best ERA at 1.86. Chicago's pitching evaporated during the World Series, however, as the A's batted .316. Bender and Coombs overpowered the Cubs' bats and led Philadelphia to an easy five-game series victory. Philadelphia's Sherry Magee was the NL's best hitter, leading in batting at .331, runs with 110, and RBIs with 123.

McGraw's Giants dynasty of the 1900s and 1910s can be divided into two distinct clubs. One was the team that won back-to-back NL flags in 1904 and 1905, won the 1905 World Series, and finished second in 1906 and 1908; this team was built around players imported from the old Orioles plus shortstop Bill Dahlen, acquired in a trade with Brooklyn. The second phase of the Giants dynasty was the team of 1911 through 1917, which was made up almost exclusively of players scouted, recruited, and groomed by McGraw himself, men like Rube Marquard, Fred Merkle, Larry Doyle, Fred Snodgrass, Art Devlin, Chief Meyers, Hooks Wiltse, Charles "Buck" Herzog, and Jeff Tesreau. The great Christy Mathewson, of course, was the mainstay of both generations of Giants—at least until 1915, when Matty burned out and went 8–14. The hallmark of the first Giants team was their epic pennant battles against the Chicago Cubs. The second team, however, will always be remembered for its penchant for postseason disaster; as dominant as they were in the regular season—this team won three consecutive pennants between 1911 and 1913—they were snakebit in the World Series.

The 1911 World Series saw the second meeting of McGraw and Mack, whose A's had failed to score a single earned run in the 1905 series. This time, however, Philadelphia won four games to two on a pair of dramatic late-inning home runs, one off Marquard and one off Mathewson, by third baseman Frank Baker. This would be nothing unusual in a modern World Series, but it caused a nationwide sensation in 1911, when home runs were so rare that Baker had led the AL with a total of only eleven. It was this pair of home runs that caused Baker to be known for the rest of his major-league career as Home Run Baker. Giants fans inaugurated a peculiarly New York tradition by electing outfielder Red Murray, who had gone 0–21 with three errors, as the series goat. From then on, almost every World Series defeat suffered by a New York team would be blamed, in the press and in the minds of the fans, at least, on a single player.

An interesting footnote to the 1911 series is the play that ended game five. In the bottom of the ninth, Doyle tagged up from third and beat outfielder Danny Murphy's throw to the plate to win the game for the Giants. Umpire Bill Klem noticed that the sliding Doyle had missed the plate and made no call; the A's, however, left the field without attempting to make any play. In a postgame interview, Philadelphia manager Connie Mack revealed that he and his team had noticed Doyle's mistake but conceded the game out of fear of the Polo Grounds crowd. "It was only three years after the Giants had lost the 1908 pennant . . . on a technicality in the famous Merkle decision," Mack explained, "These fans were joy crazed after the Giants pulled out the game the way they did, and they would have wrecked the place had Doyle been tagged out before leaving the park"[1]

In 1912 the Giants found an even more interesting way to lose, this time to the Boston Red Sox, when center fielder Fred Snodgrass dropped an easy fly ball in the tenth inning of the final game to put the tying run on base. Two runs eventually scored in the inning and Snodgrass became the goat; his play was nicknamed the $30,000 Muff, after the difference between the winning and losing team's shares. Of course, blaming Snodgrass alone was not at all fair. Costly mistakes were also made in the final game by Art Fletcher and, believe it or not, Fred Merkle. There is also the fact that immediately after his dropped fly ball, Snodgrass made an amazing circus catch to take a triple away from Harry Hooper. To his credit, McGraw handled Snodgrass the same way he had handled Merkle in 1908; he fiercely defended him in the press and gave him a hefty raise for the 1913 season.

However, when McGraw lost his third straight

series, four games to one—again to Mack and the Athletics—he was not so understanding. He publicly blamed the loss on first base coach Wilbert Robinson; somewhat irrationally, McGraw cast Robinson as the goat for supposedly missing a steal sign in one of the series games. The two men, who had been close friends dating back to their days as teammates on Ned Hanlon's Orioles clubs of the 1890s, quarreled over the play at the Giants' annual postseason party, and McGraw fired Robinson on the spot. Robinson went on to manage the Giants' crosstown rival Brooklyn Dodgers for the next 18 years.

The Giants' final dead-ball-era pennant came in 1917, but McGraw's horrible World Series streak continued as the Giants lost to the Chicago White Sox, four games to two. True to form, the Giants produced another famous goat. This time it was third baseman Heinie Zimmerman, who batted only .120 and was blamed for a botched run-down play in the sixth game in which White Sox second baseman Eddie Collins was able to score a key run.

With the passing of the dead-ball era, John McGraw's postseason luck finally turned around; the Giants won the World Series in 1921 and 1922. And McGraw continued to manage through the 1932 season, retiring with 4,879 career games managed and 2,840 wins, both second only to the ageless Connie Mack in all of baseball history. McGraw was far and away the most influential manager of the 20th century. Something of his fiery spirit lives on today in a line of teacher-pupil relationships that links The Little Napoleon to a number of modern baseball men. Casey Stengel, who played the outfield for McGraw in the early 1920s and became McGraw's protege, taught Billy Martin, who was the chief influence on two modern managers, Lou Piniella and Mike Hargrove, as well as possible managers-in-waiting Graig Nettles, Chris Chambliss, and Willie Randolph.

Few modern fans know the name of manager Frank Selee (pronounced See'-lee). Managing the Boston Beaneaters (later known as the Braves) and the Chicago Cubs in the 1890s and into the dead-ball era, Selee, who never played major-league ball, won 1,500 fewer games than John McGraw and more than 2,000 fewer than Connie Mack. Selee is not in the Baseball Hall of Fame. If a few circumstances of his career had been different, however, he may well have gone down in history as the 1890s' third great gift to 20th-century baseball.

Selee's great Boston clubs of the 1890s won five pennants to three for the Orioles of Ned Hanlon and John McGraw. Yet it is the Orioles who are remembered as the greatest dynasty of the time, and it is the Orioles who are given credit for pioneering the hard-running, hit-and-run style of play that is the chief legacy of the late 19th century. Contemporary players like John Ward, however, are more than likely to attribute these innovations to Selee's Beaneaters. Ward once said, " 'Team work in the field' used to be a prime factor in a pennant-winning team, but now 'team work at the bat' is the latest wrinkle, and the Bostons have it down fine." The phrase "team work at the bat" may sound strange to fans of modern home-run oriented baseball, but in the 1890s it meant using the stolen base, bunt, bunt-and-run, hit-and-run, and run-and-hit in a bewildering assortment of variations to conduct an all-out attack on the opposing team's defense. Although Ward named Boston outfielder Tommy McCarthy as the tactical brains of the club, it was part of Selee's managerial style to find smart players and give them an unusual amount of responsibility. Still, the *Sporting News* wrote in 1893 that "the success of the Boston team is due, more than any other thing, to a manager who is a thorough baseball general . . . who knows what should be done and how to do it, and is able to impress his advice upon the men under his control."[2]

In 1902 Selee took over the Chicago Cubs. This was a rebuilding job at least as daunting as that faced by John McGraw in New York. The talentless Cubs had finished eighth in 1899, fifth in 1900, and sixth in 1901. Like McGraw, Selee was decisive in personnel matters; he got rid of most of the Chicago veterans and moved struggling catcher Frank Chance to first base, where he would go on to have a Hall-of-Fame career. Before the season ended, he had brought in a new double-play combination of shortstop Joe Tinker and second baseman Johnny Evers. If these names sound familiar, it is because of New York sportswriter Franklin P. Adams's famous poem, inspired by the Cubs' magnificent double-play combination:

These are the saddest of possible words—
    Tinker to Evers to Chance.
Trio of Bear Cubs fleeter than birds—
    Tinker to Evers to Chance.
Thoughtlessly pricking our gonfalon bubble
    [balloon],
Making a Giant hit into a double [i.e. double
    play],
Words that are weighty with nothing but
    trouble—
    Tinker to Evers to Chance.

Selee's efforts did not produce instant victory—the Cubs finished fifth in 1902, third in 1903, and second in 1904—but they sowed a seed that would bear fruit for the rest of the dead-ball era. By 1905, Selee had added to the team catcher Johnny Kling, who was famous for throwing from the crouch à la modern catcher Benito Santiago; outfielders Jimmy Slagle and Wildfire Schulte; and pitchers Three Finger Brown and Ed Reulbach. Brown's nickname came from a farm accident that deprived him of parts of three fingers on his throwing

Cubs' second baseman Johnny Evers,
the pivotman of the famed double-play combination
of Tinker to Evers to Chance

hand but gave his curve ball an unusual, baffling break. Underrated right-handed pitcher Ed Reulbach was a steady, winning pitcher on a winning team. Consistently among the league leaders in winning percentage, he went 18–13, 19–4, 17–4, and 24–7 between 1905 and 1908; he retired in 1917 with a record of 181–105, the 11th-best career ERA of all time, 2.28, and a record of 2–0 over four World Series.

Unfortunately, Selee managed to evade most of the credit for the Cubs dynasty that he created by contracting tuberculosis in 1905. The illness forced him to turn the club over to player-manager Frank Chance, who remained at the helm during the Cubs' glory years; Selee lived until 1909, long enough to see the team he put together, little changed by Chance, win three NL pennants and two World Series. Forgotten as he is, Selee compiled the fourth-best career winning percentage in baseball history, managed the first two NL teams to win 100 games in a season, and gave a dozen future Hall-of-Famers their first big-league jobs.

THE YEAR: 1911

Both leagues adopted the cork-centered ball in 1911, bringing if not the end of the dead-ball era, then at least a brief holiday from it. Pitchers were put on the defensive and major-league runs-scored totals and batting averages shot up; the NL batted .260 and the AL .273. Two teams in the AL, Philadelphia and Detroit, batted over .290.

The New York Giants won the pennant, thanks to the league's best offense. Catcher Chief Meyers hit .332, second baseman Larry Doyle slugged 25 triples and scored 102 runs; McGraw's team scored 756 runs, one fewer than the Cubs. All this slugging didn't inhibit the Giants on the base paths. Outfielder Josh Devore stole 61 bases, second in the NL to Cincinnati's Bob

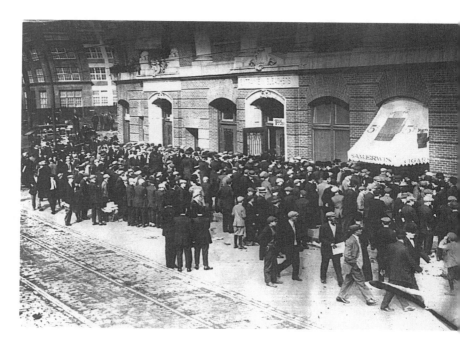

*Fans enter Shibe Park during the 1911 World Series.
Opened in 1909, Shibe Park was the first
concrete-and-steel ballpark.*

Bescher with an NL-record 81, and was followed on the leader board by teammates Fred Snodgrass at 51 and Fred Merkle at 49. Bescher's record stood until Maury Wills of the Dodgers broke it in 1962. As a team, New York swiped an all-time record 347 bases, 57 more than runner-up Cincinnati. The Giants also had the NL's best pitching staff, anchored by 26-game-winner Mathewson, who was the only NL pitcher with an ERA below 2.00 at 1.99, and Rube Marquard, who in his first full year in the rotation went 24–7 with a 2.50 ERA. Once known to New York fans as the $11,000 Lemon, Marquard was now renamed the $11,000 Beauty.

Johnny Evers's nervous breakdown in May may well have cost the Cubs the pennant, as they came in 7½ games off the pace. Chicago's Wildfire Schulte won the NL Chalmers award after leading the league in RBIs with 121 and home runs with 21, and the 37-year-old Honus Wagner won his final batting title at .334 for third-place Pittsburgh. Fourth-place Philadelphia boasted rookie sensation Pete Alexander, who at 24 years of age went 28–13 to lead the NL in wins, with seven shutouts and a 2.57 ERA.

Connie Mack's Athletics powerhouse repeated, but not without being given a run for their money by good-hit, no-pitch Detroit. Second to last in team ERA, the Tigers held first place for much of the first half of the season thanks to the fearsome duo of Crawford and Cobb, who drove in 259 runs between them. Crawford batted .378 and slugged .526. Cobb scored 147 runs and collected 248 hits, 47 doubles, 24 triples, and 83 stolen bases to put together the best offensive season by any hitter since the 1890s. Cleveland's Joe Jackson hit .408 to set the all-time rookie batting average record but did not win the batting title, as Ty Cobb batted .420; the two were the only men to break the .400-barrier between 1901 and 1920. The A's scored a league-best 861 runs and batted .296; their big gun was third baseman Home Run Baker, who drove in 115 runs.

The death of pitching legend Addie Joss from meningitis provoked an outpouring of grief all over the baseball world. A 160–97 lifetime pitcher over nine seasons with perennial non-contender Cleveland, the popular Joss left a 1.88 career ERA, the second-lowest in history.

Like that of McGraw's New York Giants, the Red Sox' dead-ball dynasty can be divided into two phases; the 1902–04 team and the 1912–18 team. Unlike the Giants, however, there was no great managerial genius behind the Red Sox. In the first phase of the Red Sox dynasty, the team consisted more or less of the core of Frank Selee's Boston Beaneaters transplanted to the new American League. The team featured ex-Beaneaters Jimmy Collins, the top defensive third baseman of the day, pitcher Big Bill Dineen, early power-hitter Buck Freeman, and outfielder Chick Stahl. Rounding out the Red Sox' starting lineup were two former St. Louis Cardinals: catcher Lou Criger and pitching great Cy Young. Managed by Collins, this team thoroughly dominated the pennant race, leading the AL in team runs, fewest runs allowed, batting average, ERA, and shutouts and coming in 14½ games ahead of Philadelphia. Even though peace had yet to be officially made between the warring major leagues, Pittsburgh owner Barney Dreyfuss and Boston owner Henry Killilea agreed to play the first modern World Series on a best of nine basis.

Cy Young or no, the Red Sox entered the series as underdogs. One reason for this was the fact that the young AL was considered to be a notch below the NL competitively; another was Fred Clarke's Pirates powerhouse, a team that had won three consecutive pennants. The Pirates' offense boasted superstar Honus Wagner and lesser stars Clarke, Ginger Beaumont, and Tommy Leach; the Pirates pitching staff was as deep as any in baseball, with Deacon Phillippe, Sam Leever, William "Brickyard" Kennedy, and Ed Doheny.

By the time of the first game, held at Boston's Huntington Avenue Grounds on October 1, local baseball fans were in a frenzy of anticipation. According to Pittsburgh outfielder Tommy Leach:

> *That was probably the wildest World Series ever played. Arguing all the time between the teams, between the players and the umpires, and especially between the players and the fans. That's*

the truth. The fans were part of the game in those days. They'd pour right out onto the field and argue with the players and umpires. Was sort of hard to keep the game going sometimes, to say the least."[3]

After four games Boston was down, three games to one, with the next three games scheduled for Pittsburgh. It was then that the Royal Rooters began to serenade the Pirates with the popular song "Tessie." The Royal Rooters were a group of fanatical Boston fans who had defected from the Beaneaters to the AL along with so many of their favorites. They followed the team at home and on the road, sitting together in a section of the stands and leading synchronized cheers or playing music. During game five of the 1903 series the Royal Rooters hit upon the idea of singing "Tessie" with new lyrics designed to irritate every member of the Pirates in turn. Instead of "Tessie, you make me feel so badly, Why don't you turn around?" they sang: "Honus, why do you hit so badly, Take a back seat and sit down," and so on. When the Red Sox won game five, 11-2, the Rooters figured that they were onto something and continued the "Tessie" attack, nonstop, for the rest of the series. Sure enough, Boston won the next two games, 6-3 and 7-3; returning home for game eight, they finished off the Pirates as Big Bill Dineen threw a four-hit shutout and won, 3-0. Did "Tessie" really have anything to do with it? Reminiscing about the series in Lawrence Ritter's oral history *The Glory of Their Times,* Tommy Leach admitted that it was a possibility. "[The song] sort of got on your nerves after a while," he said, "And before we knew what happened, we'd lost the World Series."

The Red Sox of 1912 to 1918 were an incredible fount of baseball talent that not only produced four pennant winners, but also provided the foundation of the great New York Yankees dynasty of the 1920s. The 1912 Red Sox, the club that became the beneficiary of Snodgrass's "$30,000 Muff," were built around one of the greatest defensive outfields in major-league history. Duffy Lewis excelled at scampering up "Duffy's Cliff" (the predecessor of the Green Monster) in left, Harry Hooper covered right, and Hall-of-Famer Tris Speaker played his usual, daringly shallow center. Speaker hit .383 in 1912, with 53 doubles and 10 homers, and in over 22 years in the AL he compiled a lifetime batting average of .344, the seventh-best ever. Pitching for the 1912 Sox was Colorado-born fastballer "Smokey" Joe Wood, who put together one of the century's greatest pitching seasons, going 34–5 with a 1.91 ERA.

In the five years that followed, Boston won three more World Series and developed many of the biggest stars of the 1910s, among them pitchers Ernie Shore, George "Rube" Foster, Babe Ruth, Carl Mays, and Waite Hoyt, as well as everyday players like shortstop Everett Scott and catcher Wally Schang. Under owner Harry Frazee, however, the man who bought the Red Sox in 1918, nearly all of these players were sold or traded to the New York Yankees in what is still remembered in Boston as "The Rape of the Red Sox." In 1918 Frazee did make one positive, if indirect, contribution to baseball when he hired Ed Barrow to replace his manager, Jack Barry, who had been drafted to serve in World War I. This is the same Barrow who had signed Honus Wagner to a minor-league contract. In an effort to squeeze the most out of the war-shortened Red Sox roster, Barrow hit upon the idea of playing starting pitcher Babe Ruth in the outfield between starts. This was not an easy call; Ruth was one of the team's best pitchers, having gone 23–12 and 24–13 over the previous two years. The experiment worked; in between going 13–7 in 19 starts in 1918, Ruth hit a league-leading 11 home runs in only 95 at bats. The following year Barrow all but stopped pitching Ruth, and the young left-hander belted an all-time record 29 home runs. Frazee immediately sold him to the Yankees, where he altered the course of baseball history forever.

THE YEAR: 1912

Both major leagues reached offensive peaks for the decade in 1912. The NL hit .272, the AL hit .265, and there was an explosion of triples; three of the all-time top 10 triples seasons came in 1912: Cobb's 23, tied for 10th; Joe Jackson's 26, tied for second; and Pittsburgh outfielder Owen Wilson's major-league record 36.

Cubs third baseman Heinie Zimmerman was the league's best hitter and led in doubles with 41, RBIs with 103, home runs with 14, and batting at .372. He lost out in the Chalmers voting, however, to New York's Larry Doyle. Doyle's .330 average, Red Murray's 20 triples and 92 RBIs, and Fred Merkle's 11 home runs paced a tough, versatile Giants team that stole a league-high 319 bases and scored 823 runs. Christy Mathewson went 23–12 and once again New York had the only NL pitcher to break the 2.00 ERA mark: 23-year-old spitball specialist Jeff Tesreau at 1.96. Rube Marquard won 26 games, 19 of them coming in a consecutive-win streak that lasted from April 11 to July 3; this tied the 19th-century record set by another Giant, Tim Keefe, in 1888.

The Boston Red Sox demolished their competition in the AL and went 105–47, 14 games better than Washington. The Senators had been lifted single-handedly out of the second division by Walter Johnson, who went 33–12 with a league-leading 1.39 ERA. Johnson and Smokey Joe Wood, who went 34–5 with ten shut-outs for the Red Sox, engaged in a personal battle over the AL record for consecutive pitching victories. In early

September, Wood had 13 straight victories and was threatening Johnson's record of 16—set early that same season—when he met Johnson himself face to face in a dramatic showdown. Wood came out on top in a tight pitcher's duel, 1-0, and went on to tie the record.

AL Chalmers award winner Tris Speaker put together a 30-game hitting streak. Ty Cobb hit .410, his second straight year over .400, in spite of an early-season suspension for attacking a disabled heckler in a New York grandstand.

The 1912 World Series was a thrilling eight-game contest that featured a tie (called by darkness); great defense, including Red Sox outfielder Harry Hooper's bare-hand catch of an apparent Larry Doyle home run; and Fred Snodgrass's critical dropped fly ball in the tenth inning of game eight that paved the way for Boston's series-winning rally.

Today, few fans, even Oakland Athletics fans, know why Athletics players wear a patch with an embroidered white elephant on their uniform. It all goes back to 1902, when John McGraw ripped the young American League, its founder Ban Johnson, and the owner of its Philadelphia franchise, Connie Mack. "In Philadelphia," he told reporters, "[Connie Mack] has a white elephant on his hands." During the two decades that followed, Mack and his team adopted the white elephant, a symbol of conspicuous uselessness, as their mascot and made John McGraw eat his words. Not only did the A's win five dead-ball-era pennants to equal McGraw's Giants, they defeated the Giants head-to-head in two out of their three World Series meetings.

Like McGraw, Connie Mack was a second-generation Irishman who had played in the rowdy NL of the 19th century; Mack was a bare-handed catcher for Washington in the 1880s and a player-manager for Pittsburgh in the 1890s. That is where all similarity

Connie Mack (left) poses with the Giants'
John McGraw. The consummate gentleman,
Mack managed the Philadelphia A's for 50 seasons
(1901–1950), guiding the team to nine pennants
and five world championships.

between the two ends. Mack was a shrewd game manager who was capable of great innovation and courage, but he took a much more gentlemanly approach than the feisty McGraw. He never browbeat or publicly criticized his players and inspired almost universal loyalty and respect. In 1910, the A's players chipped in and bought Mack his first car. He managed to get the most out of solid citizens like Eddie Collins and odd, unreliable characters like pitcher Rube Waddell, who won 130 games for Mack over six seasons, but invariably self-destructed in his brief stints with four other major-league clubs. A tall, thin man with a kind face, Mack managed in a suit, tie, and straw hat; he had no need of a uniform because he never left the bench to berate an umpire.

Mack had no known vices. He was soft-spoken and a bit prudish; his players called him "Mr. Mack" and watched their language when he was within earshot. Nevertheless, as his handling of McGraw's white elephant remark shows, he had a sly sense of humor. In a game during the 1940s, the story goes, slick-fielding A's first baseman Ferris Fain charged and fielded a sacrifice bunt and, in an attempt to get a runner going to third base, threw the ball into left field. Two runs scored on the play. When he returned to the dugout, Mack asked him why he had thrown to third. "What am I supposed to do with the ball?" Fain said sarcastically, "shove it up my ass?" To which Mack answered, "Well, young man, it would have done less harm there."

Mack was as good a judge of talent as McGraw, but he considered character and education as well as playing ability. Mack pioneered the signing of college players, and it was on college campuses that he uncovered such stars as Eddie Plank, Chief Bender, Jack Coombs, Jack Barry, and Eddie Collins. Along with first baseman John "Stuffy" McInnis and third baseman

Home Run Baker, shortstop Barry and second baseman Collins formed what would become known as Philadelphia's "$100,000 infield." (The $100,000 was supposed to signify an unimaginably large sum of money.) With the addition of hard-hitting outfielders Danny Murphy and Rube Oldring and a formidable pitching staff of Bender, Plank, and Coombs, Mack won four of the five pennants between 1910 and 1914. In the World Series he defeated the two greatest NL dynasties of the era: the Giants of Mathewson, Marquard, Meyers, and Doyle; and the Cubs of Brown, Reulbach, Tinker, Evers, and Chance.

In 1914, however, Connie Mack suffered a rare lapse in judgment. He had been swept, four games to none, in the World Series by the so-called Miracle Braves, a team that he considered far inferior to his Athletics. Managed by the brilliant and somewhat obnoxious George Stallings, the Braves had risen from last place in July to win the NL flag by 10½ games; this is still the biggest comeback in baseball history. Mack was irritated that some of his players were negotiating behind his back with teams from the Federal League (FL), a newly formed would-be major league. That, combined with the series loss to Stallings, whom Mack strongly disliked, drove him over the edge. In a fit of pique, Mack sold off his stars to the highest bidder in the off-season. Ironically, their selling prices added up to about $100,000. Eddie Collins went to Charles Comiskey's White Sox for $50,000 and helped build the great Chicago teams of 1917 to 1920; Barry went to the Red Sox; Home Run Baker went to the Yankees. Mack released Plank and Bender, who promptly defected to the FL. When the dust cleared, the Athletics were a last-place club. And that is where they finished for the next eight seasons.

Thanks to his part-ownership of the team, Mack was able to survive this debacle and live to fight again with a rebuilt Athletics dynasty that won consecutive pennants in 1929, 1930, and 1931. Connie Mack, however, did not stop there; he eventually gained majority ownership of the Athletics. Ten years older than John McGraw, he continued to manage 18 years after McGraw's retirement and 16 years after McGraw's death, setting the all-time records for most games managed, 7,878; most wins, 3,776; and most losses, 4,025. In 1950, his final season, Mack could still be seen sitting at the end of the A's bench, wearing the suit, straw hat, and high celluloid collar that were in fashion in the days before Babe Ruth, and gently positioning his outfielders with a wave of his scorecard. Baseball's answer to the giant redwood tree, Connie Mack managed an incredible 53 major-league seasons. He played against Cap Anson and managed pitcher Bobby Shantz, who retired in 1964. Born during Abraham Lincoln's second year in the White House, he died during the Eisenhower administration in 1956, 93 years later.

CHAPTER
SEVEN

Palaces of the Fans: The First Ballparks Built to Last

Major-league baseball was a booming business in the dead-ball era. There were a lot of reasons for this. The two-league, 16-team format made baseball available to nearly every major population center. Under Ban Johnson's influence, major-league baseball lived down the reputation for fan violence and rowdy, dirty on-field play that it had acquired in the late 19th century; respect for umpires was at an all-time high. The annual World Series provided baseball with a brilliant national showcase; each season, the epic October battles between the Giants, Athletics, Red Sox, and Cubs attracted more and more fan interest. Finally, between 1890 and 1920, nearly every major-league city legalized Sunday baseball, opening up the game to unprecedented numbers of working-class fans; many clubs made most or all of their yearly profit from Sunday afternoon games. The last holdouts were Boston, which first allowed Sunday baseball in 1929, and Pennsylvania, which finally allowed Pittsburgh and Philadelphia to play on Sunday in 1934.

126

For all these reasons, ticket sales skyrocketed in the 1900s and continued to rise, though more slowly, during the 1910s. Total major-league attendance exceeded 100 million for the two dead-ball decades, or an average of around a half million per season for each team; this represented an increase of more than 100 percent from 1890s levels.

There was no doubt that baseball was growing rich, but it had a big problem: the ballparks. In spite of baseball's expanding crowds and expanding coffers, major-league games were still being played in slapdash wooden structures that were more suited to a rodeo or a Wild West show. Thrown together with little attention to aesthetics or fan comfort, these wooden parks had burned down with regularity throughout the 1890s; in 1894 alone, 30 percent of all big-league parks went up in smoke. By the late 1900s, the situation was becoming downright dangerous. It was one thing to have a grandstand collapse or catch fire with 500 people in the park; it was quite another when there were 20,000. In 1908 the *Sporting Life* observed, "It looks as though ball parks now in existence would be all too small for the multitudes ten years from now. . . . On some grounds— like the Cub park, for instance—the limit has been reached in seating capacity."[1]

The first man to see the solution was Ben Shibe, the creative part-owner of the Philadelphia Athletics and a manufacturer of baseballs. In 1909 he took advantage of new reinforced concrete technology to build the first-ever concrete-and-steel baseball facility. He called it Shibe Park. When it opened on April 12, 1909, a huge crowd of 30,000 A's fans saw a monumental structure that looked more like an opera house or a museum than a place to play ball. The ornamental facade of brick, trimmed with concrete reliefs, was decked with colorful banners and flags. Above the entrance was a three-story tower, topped by a French Renaissance cupola that housed manager Connie Mack's office. When they walked inside, the fans had their breath taken away by the majestic sweep of Shibe Park's three decks and the great green expanse of its immense outfield; the center field fence was 515 feet from home plate. In a concession to the increasingly popular automobile, Shibe provided 400 parking spaces.

The *Sporting Life* wrote, prophetically, that "[Shibe Park] has inaugurated a new era in baseball." The A's new home was more than just a new kind of building; because of its beauty and comfort, it soon became an attraction in itself—as have modern parks like Baltimore's Camden Yards and Toronto's Skydome. Like these ultra-modern parks, Shibe Park and its descendants made their tenants even richer. And as with Camden Yards and the other wonderful new ballparks of the 1990s, as soon as Shibe's fellow baseball owners saw his new park, they wanted one for themselves.

THE YEAR: 1913

Possibly because of increased use of the spitball and other trick pitches, major-league pitchers somehow began to regain their mastery over hitters in 1913. The cork-centered baseball of 1911 was still in use, but runs scored plummeted, and the days of the sub-2.00 ERA returned.

In a miserable, foul-smelling corner of Brooklyn known as Pigtown, Dodgers owner Charles Ebbets constructed Ebbets Field, the team's home for the next 44 years. Fittingly, considering the Dodgers' penchant for goofy mistakes, Ebbets discovered on Opening Day that he had forgotten to build a flagpole or a press box.

For the second year in a row, the New York Giants won more than 100 games and ended the pennant race before the weather got hot. McGraw's team combined an overachieving, starless lineup with three of the five best pitchers in the NL: Christy Mathewson, who won the league ERA title at 2.06, 23-game-winner Rube Marquard, and the spitballing Tesreau, who finished third in ERA at 2.17. The only Giants hitter to show up on a leader board was outfielder George Burns, who hit 37 doubles and led the NL in strikeouts with 74. Yet Merkle, Meyers, Doyle, and the rest of the New York line-up managed to score 684 runs, third-best in the league. Home-run sensation Clifford "Gavvy" Cravath turned in the year's best offensive season for second-place Philadelphia. He led the league in RBIs with 128, homers with 19, and slugging average at .568; his .341 batting average was second to Chalmers award–winner Jake Daubert, who hit .350 for Brooklyn.

With career years from Eddie Collins, who led the league in runs with 125, Home Run Baker, who batted .336 and drove in 126 runs, and Stuffy McInnis, who hit .326, Philadelphia won its third AL pennant in four years, finishing 96–57, 6½ games ahead of Washington—or, to be more accurate, 6½ games ahead of Walter Johnson. The Big Train had his finest season in 1913, winning 36 and losing only 7 and leading the league in wins, ERA, strikeouts, fewest hits per game, and nearly everything else. He threw 11 of his career 110 shutouts that year and pitched a record 55⅔ consecutive scoreless innings; his 1.09 ERA is the third-best in modern history. With the Senators playing .837 ball with their ace on the mound (and .486 without him), Johnson became the first and only pitcher to win a Chalmers award.

Once again, Ty Cobb at .390 and Joe Jackson at .373 came in first and second in the batting race. Jackson led the league in doubles with 39 and Detroit's Sam Crawford banged out a league-high 23 triples, but Cleveland and Detroit were never in the race. An

*AL greats (left to right) Ty Cobb, Joe Jackson, and
Sam Crawford confer before a game.*

up-and-coming White Sox staff, including Ewell
"Reb" Russell, Ed Cicotte, and Jim Scott, compiled the
league's lowest ERA at 2.33.

In a repeat of 1911, Philadelphia defeated the
Giants in the World Series, but this time they did the
job in only five games. A's pitchers Chief Bender, Joe
Bush, and Eddie Plank had an easy time of it against
a New York line-up depleted by injuries to Merkle,
Snodgrass, and Meyers. The Giants' pitching fell apart;
Marquard had a series ERA of 7.00, Al Demaree 4.50,
and Tesreau 6.48. The lone exception was Christy
Mathewson, who pitched two complete games, winning

New York's only victory and allowing only two earned runs in 19 innings.

The second concrete-and-steel ballpark was Pittsburgh's Forbes Field, which was opened by Pirates owner Barney Dreyfuss only a few months later than Shibe Park, in June 1909. Slightly smaller than the new Philadelphia ballpark, Forbes was, by all accounts, more comfortable and even more beautiful. It featured ramps to make for easy access to the stands, elevators that lifted the wealthy to luxury boxes on the third deck, and spacious, modern locker rooms for both teams and the umpiring crew. Elegant terra-cotta tiles adorned the exterior, and the top deck had an attractive slate roof. Although at first the project was mocked in the press as "Dreyfuss's Folly" and, as Dreyfuss later recalled, "a friend bet me a $150 suit that we would never fill the park," Opening Day at Forbes Field drew a crowd of 30,338—some 5,000 more than its official capacity. So many businessmen played hooky and went to the game that it felt like Sunday morning instead of a weekday afternoon in downtown Pittsburgh.

It did not take long for the other owners to get the message. Before the 1909 season ended, League Park in Cleveland and Sportsman's Park in St. Louis had been renovated using concrete and steel. In 1910 Chicago's palatial Comiskey Park went up; 1911 saw the arrival of Griffith Stadium in Washington, D.C., and the new concrete-and-steel Polo Grounds in New York City. Redland Field in Cincinnati, Navin Field (now Tiger Stadium) in Detroit, and Fenway Park in Boston opened in 1912. In 1913 the Brooklyn Dodgers built Ebbets Field. When the Chicago Cubs moved into Weeghman Park (now Wrigley Field) at the conclusion of the Federal League War and the Boston Braves built Braves Field in 1915, virtually every major-league club was playing in a concrete-and-steel ballpark.

The new ballparks of the dead-ball era were far more deserving of the title "palaces of the fans" than the finest of the tiny wooden parks of the 1880s. And, unlike the huge fire traps of the 1890s, they left their mark on the game. First, they were monuments, shrines of baseball that became a central part of the fan experience. No one missed the ballparks that preceded them. Three of the ballparks of the dead-ball days, however, remain in use and are so beloved to this day that their owners are afraid to replace them for fear of alienating the fans. Many of those that have fallen victim to the wrecking ball are still mourned. It is certainly no accident that Camden Yards, Cleveland's Jacobs Field, and Chicago's new Comiskey Park call to mind the parks that were built between 1909 and 1915.

Second, in cramming the new ballparks into sometimes odd-shaped city lots, the designers of the first concrete-and-steel parks were often forced to bring in outfield fences and create short porches, strange angles, and other asymmetries. As these new ballparks drew more fans and added more decks and bleachers in order to increase seating capacity, their urban setting forced them to expand inward by moving outfield fences closer to home plate; this had tremendous unforeseen consequences when Babe Ruth and other hitters of the 1920s found that they could reach these shortened fences by swatting long fly balls.

Finally, because the owners invested so much money to build them, the ballparks of 1909–15 brought about an era of unprecedented stability in major-league baseball. As recent history has shown, club owners do not hesitate to leave publicly owned ballparks for greener pastures; it is quite another thing, however, for an owner to leave a ballpark that he has paid for. As major-league clubs stopped relocating to other cities, they became closely identified not only with their parks but with particular urban neighborhoods. When

Brooklyn Dodgers team announcer Red Barber was offered a raise to go to work for the Yankees in the 1940s, he refused, later explaining, "I had roots. I loved the borough. . . . I loved the park." This is a sentiment that could only have been expressed in the post–World War I era. The concrete-and-steel building boom of the 1900s and 1910s inaugurated a half century in which nearly all of the 16 major-league teams remained at the same home address. They played in the same cities, in the same parks—even under the same names; team nicknames, which for most of baseball history had been discarded every few years or so, virtually stopped changing around this time. Fans took their children to watch the same team that their grandparents had rooted for, in the same park that their parents had taken them to. It is no wonder that baseball has never really gotten over its nostalgia for those days.

CHAPTER EIGHT

Tip-Tops and Terrapins: Monopoly War V and the Federal League

Anyone who knew the history of baseball, going back to William Hulbert and the beginning of the major-league monopoly, could have seen it coming. The more prosperous the baseball business became in the dead-ball era, the more it attracted the attention of millionaire investors who wanted to get in on the action. Conditions were ripe for another monopoly war. As baseball writer Ernie Lanigan put it:

> Baseball . . . began to get noticeably popular and profitable [in the late 1900s] and in the winter of 1913 there was a general impression that all one had to do in order to make a fortune was to erect a ball park in a major league city, hire some major leaguers and some Class AA men, announce the formation of a new league—and then sit back and divide the profits.[1]

Monopoly War V, or the Federal League War, had most of the basic elements shared by Monopoly Wars I through IV. The Federal League began as a minor league. In late 1913 it named James Gilmore, a man who had grown rich in the stationery business, as league president. During the off-season of 1913–14, Gilmore plotted with a group of rich friends to establish the Federal League as a third major league. The group included Charles Weeghman, who owned a chain of lunch counters—the pre–World War I equivalent of a modern fast food chain; St. Louis brewer Otto Steifel; ice machine manufacturer Phil Ball, also from St. Louis; and Brooklynite Robert Ward, the manufacturer of Tip Top bread. In 1915 oil magnate Harry Sinclair came on board. Sinclair later became the central figure in the Teapot Dome affair, a scandal that ruined the Warren Harding presidency in the early 1920s. The Federal League recruited experienced baseball men John Ward and Ned Hanlon as advisors. Like Ban Johnson in 1901, FL president Gilmore first attempted to negotiate major-league status for his league peacefully, but the uncrowned "czar" of organized baseball—the same Ban Johnson—rejected him out of hand in 1914.

The Federal League responded by declaring war. It put four FL franchises in major-league cities: the Chicago Whales, the Brooklyn Tip-Tops—nominated by many writers as the worst team nickname ever—the Pittsburgh Stogies, and the St. Louis Terriers; and four in cities with clubs in the high minors: the Indianapolis Hoosiers, the Baltimore Terrapins, the Buffalo Blues, and the Kansas City Packers. In 1915 Indianapolis was dropped and replaced by Harry Sinclair's Newark, New Jersey, Peppers; the plan was to relocate the Newark team to New York City in 1916. Following precedent, the FL attempted to lure as many major leaguers as possible with fat, long-term contracts that did not include the reserve clause.

This tactic was a limited success. A few big-name major leaguers did jump to the FL, including former

Cubs shortstop Joe Tinker, who had resented being sold by Cincinnati to Brooklyn for several times the amount of his annual salary; star first baseman Hal Chase; and, of course, former A's Chief Bender and Eddie Plank. But the AL and NL owners had to lay out tremendous amounts of cash to buy the loyalty of the many players who did not jump. Superstars Walter Johnson and Ty Cobb got raises of $5,500 and $8,000, respectively. Lesser players also benefited. For instance, the Chicago White Sox tore up third baseman Buck Weaver's contract for $2,500 and replaced it with a three-year deal at $6,000 per.

THE YEAR: 1914

Nineteen-hundred-and-fourteen belonged to the Miracle Braves, baseball's all-time comeback kids, who rose from last place in July to a world championship in October. Starting the season with a 4–18 record and missing the soul of the team, injured shortstop Walter "Rabbit" Maranville, fiery Braves manager George Stallings had his work cut out. Credited by many historians with having pioneered the use of platooning, Stallings transformed his team into a hustling, running, clutch-hitting machine by midsummer. The Braves won eight straight in early July, part of a 34-10 stretch that pulled them up to fourth place; nine straight wins later they were within seven games of front-running New York; and on August 10, they found themselves in second place heading into a three-game make-or-break series with the Giants. The Braves swept John McGraw's Giants, roared into the lead in early September, and sprinted to a 94–59 record, 10½ games up on New York.

Stallings's team hit a mediocre .251, had only one .300 hitter, outfielder Joe Connolly, and were fourth in team ERA at 2.74. How did they win? One answer is patient hitting; they drew a league-leading 502 bases on balls. Former Cub Johnny Evers was the team leader with a .390 on-base average. They also played great defense. Chalmers winner Evers led all second basemen in fielding and runner-up Maranville led in double plays; Maranville also set an NL record for put outs and the still-unbroken single-season major-league record for total chances at shortstop. The tough-as-nails Maranville, who would later teach a young, fellow French Canadian–American named Leo Durocher how to play shortstop, drove in 78 runs to lead the team. Finally, the New York Giants, who occupied first place for almost five months, ran out of gas and left the door open for Boston. The great Christy Mathewson finally looked old in 1914, winning 20 games for the last time and turning in an ERA above 3.00 for the first time in 14 full seasons. The New York hitters, led by George Burns's league-high 100 runs and 62 stolen bases, slumped late in the season.

In Philadelphia, Gavvy Cravath repeated his 19-home-run performance of 1913, and a young Brooklyn outfielder named Charles "Casey" Stengel hit .316 and led the NL in on-base average at .404.

In the AL, Chalmers winner Eddie Collins was second in batting at .344 as Connie Mack's A's took their fourth flag in five years, going 99–53 to defeat Boston. The Red Sox had the league's best ERA at 2.35 in spite of the loss of Smokey Joe Wood, who was limited to 18 games by the arm injury that would end his pitching career by 1916. Boston's young Ernie Shore had a 10–4 record with an ERA of 1.89, and Robert "Dutch" Leonard went 19–5 with history's lowest-ever seasonal ERA, 1.01.

The underdog Braves swept the World Series, 4–0, from Philadelphia and provoked Connie Mack to auction off his stars to the highest bidder. Former A's pitching star Rube Waddell died on April Fool's Day at the age of 37. He had contracted pneumonia after coming to the aid of a group of men trying to repair a levee breached by a flooding Kentucky river.

Pirates great Honus Wagner and Cleveland's Larry Lajoie both got their 3,000th major-league hit in 1914. Depending on which encyclopedia you use, they were either the first to reach the 3,000-hit plateau or the first since 19th-century legend Cap Anson.

While the Federal League failed to attract the cream of the major-league crop, either in an athletic or a moral sense—an unsettling number of FL jumpers, including Claude Hendrix, Benny Kauff, Hal Chase, and Lee Magee, were later banned from baseball for corruption—things looked good for the Federal League at the close of the 1914 season. The well-heeled FL backers were absorbing the new league's inevitable operating losses without complaint. On the field, the FL gave fans their money's worth with a thrilling pennant race and exciting individual performances. Indianapolis won a squeaker over Chicago by 1½ games; all eight FL clubs finished within 25 games of first place. Indianapolis star Benny Kauff was the Lajoie of the new league, leading all hitters in runs with 120 and doubles with 44; he won the batting title with an average of .370.

The 1915 FL season was even better, as Chicago won an exciting race in which only 16 games separated the first- and seventh-place clubs. Charles Weeghman's Chicago Whales beat out Phil Ball's St. Louis Terriers by less than a game: .566 to .565. Pittsburgh came in third, a half game out. Once again, Benny Kauff won the batting title, with a .342 average.

The AL and NL had kept most of their players in the fold by raising their salaries or threatening them with blacklisting, but they were less successful in their attempts to bring back those who did jump. Several owners went to court to prevent their reserved players from playing for the FL, but, as in the 19th century, the courts consistently refused to enforce the reserve clause. The case of Hal Chase was typical. Following the 1913 season, Chase released himself from the White Sox, using the owners' infamous 10 days' notice clause, and jumped to FL Buffalo. Chicago sued and the case landed in federal court, where judge Herbert Bissell blasted organized baseball for setting up "a species of quasi peonage unlawfully controlling and interfering with the personal freedom of the men employed." As others followed Chase, organized baseball continued to strike out in the courts; not a single player was ever compelled by court order to return to his AL or NL club.

The FL lawyers were busy, too. In January 1915 the FL owners sued organized baseball under the Sherman Antitrust Act, seeking to have the court declare the major-league monopoly illegal and order its dissolution. They chose to bring their suit in the northern district of Illinois before Judge Kenesaw Mountain Landis. The FL owners knew that Landis was a famous trust buster who had leveled the largest monetary fine—$29.4 million, later reduced on appeal—in the history of antitrust law against John D. Rockefeller's Standard Oil Company. What they did not know, however, was that Landis was a rabid baseball fan who never missed a Chicago Cubs game. Landis had no intention of dissolving organized baseball. He scoffed at an FL attorney's characterization of baseball playing as "labor," and warned that "any blows at the thing called baseball would be regarded by this court as a blow to a national institution." Knowing that the law was on the FL's side, however, Landis reserved judgment in the case. He continued to reserve judgment all summer long and into the fall.

THE YEAR: 1915

1915 brought major-league fans another Boston-Philadelphia World Series, but this time it was the Boston Red Sox against a surprising Philadelphia

Phillies team that had jumped from sixth to first in one year. Boston's deep pitching staff dominated the Phillies' batters, holding slugger Gavvy Cravath to a pair of hits and the entire lineup to a .182 batting average. The Red Sox' outfield duo of Harry Hooper, who hit .350, and Duffy Lewis, who drove in a team-high five runs, provided the punch as Philadelphia went down, four games to one.

After getting off to an 8–0 spurt, the Phillies fended off an early-season challenge from a Chicago team that featured three of the NL's top four sluggers in Fred "Cy" Williams, Wildfire Schulte, and Vic Saier, who combined for 36 home runs. Playing in brand-new Braves Field, the Boston Braves put on another late-season drive, but there was no repeat of the miracle of 1914; the team finished with a record of 83–69, seven games back. Philadelphia had the NL's best offense thanks to career years from outfielder Cravath and first baseman Fred Luderus. Cravath set the 20th-century record for home runs with 24 and led the NL in runs with 89, RBIs with 115, and bases on balls with 86; Luderus was second in the NL in hitting at .315 and second in doubles with 36. Rookie shortstop Dave "Beauty" Bancroft captained the Phillies' defense and contributed 85 runs and 77 bases on balls. Pete Alexander's 31–10 record and league-leading 1.22 ERA paced the league's best pitching staff, rounded out by 21-game winner Erskine Mayer, Al Demaree, and Eppa Rixey. The Phillies had a team ERA of only 2.17. Pittsburgh's Max Carey led the league in stolen bases with 36, winning the second of his ten stolen-base crowns. The last-place Giants continued to disintegrate; New York's only bright spot was Larry Doyle, who won the batting title at .320.

The AL pennant race came down to Boston's arms versus Detroit's bats; the Red Sox won in a squeaker, by 2½ games. Five Boston starters reached double figures in wins, including righties Rube Foster (19–8) and Ernie

Shore (19–8), and lefties Babe Ruth (18–8) and Dutch Leonard (15–7). Pitching out of the bullpen and in great pain, Joe Wood led the AL in winning percentage at .750 and ERA at 1.49, just ahead of 28-game winner Walter Johnson at 1.55. Shore was third in ERA at 1.64. Realizing that his pitching career was over, the versatile Wood returned to the minors as an outfielder; he fought his way back to the majors four years later and retired in 1922 with a lifetime .283 batting average. The Tigers nearly overcame a mediocre pitching staff of Harry Coveleski, Hooks Dauss, and four or five warm bodies by scoring an AL-best 778 runs. Bobby Veach and Sam Crawford tied for the AL RBI lead with 112; Veach swatted 40 doubles and Crawford 19 triples; and Ty Cobb won yet another batting title at .369. Cobb combined 118 walks, 208 hits, and a record 96 stolen bases to score 144 runs. Cobb's stolen-base record was to last until 1962, when the Dodgers' Maury Wills stole 104.

Albert Spalding, the sporting goods magnate and baseball executive, died of a stroke at his California home at the age of 65. Spalding was a self-made man whose life paralleled the growth of baseball from a regional amateur pastime to a wealthy and respected national institution. An Illinois farm boy who had learned the "New York game" from returning Civil War veterans, Spalding went on to win 200 games as a major-league pitcher. After making millions manufacturing baseballs, gloves, and bats, he bought and operated the Chicago Cubs, organized the worldwide baseball tour of 1888 and 1889, and led the National League to victory over the Players League in Monopoly War III. Later in life, he ran unsuccessfully for the U.S. Senate. Newspaper obituaries called Spalding "The Father of Baseball" and "in many respects the greatest man the National Game has produced."

In 1915, sportswriter Ring Lardner published the famous baseball short story "Alibi Ike" in the *Saturday*

141

Young Red Sox southpaw Babe Ruth loosens up before a game. Before he became baseball's greatest slugger, Ruth was a highly effective pitcher, posting 89 wins against 46 losses.

Evening Post, a national magazine. This was followed a year later by a baseball novel, *You Know Me, Al.* Written in colorful ballplayer slang, Lardner's stories gave fans a decidedly unidealized portrait of their major-league heroes as shallow, uneducated bumpkins with oversized egos. Unlike the one-dimensional virtuous heroes of most turn-of-the-century sports fiction, many of Lardner's ballplayers swore, chased women, and drank too much. The model for the central character of many of his stories, star pitcher Jack Keefe, was Chicago White Sox pitcher Ed Walsh, who was described by one writer as the only man on earth who could strut while standing still. Lardner's stories have been admired outside the baseball world—by world-class authors like F. Scott Fitzgerald, Virginia Woolf, and John O'Hara—and influenced the novelist Ernest Hemingway.

While the baseball world awaited the Landis decision in the Federal League antitrust suit, things began to go wrong for the FL. Operating losses piled up, made worse by a downturn in the national economy. Robert Ward had lost $700,000; total losses by FL backers came to a reported $2.5 million. Then, on October 15, 1915, Robert Ward died of rheumatism, leaving an increasingly nervous Harry Sinclair as the FL's sole remaining financial heavyweight.

With Ward's death and both sides losing millions, and with many people expecting the U.S. to enter World War I at any minute, the FL and organized baseball decided that it was time to cut a deal. As in the settlements of earlier wars with the Union Association and the Players League, the established major leagues bought off the major backers of the new league. The AL and NL paid FL owners $600,000 to dissolve the league, and an additional $129,150 to buy the contracts of the top FL stars. The New York Giants paid $50,000 of this amount for star Benny Kauff alone. The

143

antitrust suit in judge Landis's court was dropped. Finally, Charles Weeghman was allowed to buy the NL Chicago Cubs and Phil Ball was allowed to buy the St. Louis Browns in the AL. Weeghman's first move was to move the Cubs to the brand-new, concrete-and-steel ballpark that he had built for his FL Whales; this is the park that is now known as Wrigley Field. The Federal League was dead, and Monopoly War V, the last serious attempt to create a third major baseball league, was over.

Two of the most lasting legacies of Monopoly War V involved the city of Baltimore. The economic battle between the FL Baltimore Terrapins and the Baltimore Orioles, which had been one of the country's strongest minor-league franchises before 1914, drained the Orioles so badly that owner Jack Dunn was forced to sell his prize possession, 19-year-old pitcher George Herman Ruth. Ruth went along with two other players to the Boston Red Sox for a combination of cash and forgiveness of earlier debts. Had Ruth remained in Baltimore, or had he been sold to a different major-league club, there is no telling if he ever would have been converted from pitching to the outfield, where he changed the course of baseball history.

Secondly, the peace treaty that ended Monopoly War V outraged the owners of the FL Baltimore Terrapins, who were stiffed in the financial settlement and left without a club or a league when their bid to buy the NL St. Louis Cardinals was rejected. In September 1917, the Terrapins' owners filed their own antitrust suit against organized baseball. It was in the U.S. Supreme Court ruling in this case, issued five years later, that Justice Oliver Wendell Holmes made his famous argument that baseball was somehow not a business and, therefore, not subject to federal antitrust laws. It is because of Holmes's 1922 ruling that organized baseball remains a protected monopoly to this day, exempt from laws that all other businesses—and all other professional sports—must follow. And it is partially because of this exemption that in the 75 years since, no new would-be major league has dared to take on organized baseball by starting Monopoly War VI.

THE YEAR: 1916

Wilbert Robinson's Brooklyn club won its first pennant since the days of Ned Hanlon, as the beloved Zach Wheat batted .312 with 32 doubles and 13 triples. Wheat, Jake Daubert, and outfielder Hy Myers combined to give Brooklyn the league's second-best offense; only the Giants scored more runs, 597 to 585. Carried by Pete Alexander's 33 victories and league-leading 1.55 ERA, second-place Philadelphia finished 2½ games off the pace.

The strangest team in baseball was McGraw's chameleonlike Giants, who after opening the season with eight straight home losses, put together a 17-game winning streak on the road. They then slumped so badly that McGraw attempted to rebuild the team in midseason. He put young outfielder Dave Robertson into the lineup, released veteran catcher Chief Meyers, traded Larry Doyle to Chicago for legendary hot-head Heinie Zimmerman—a .295 lifetime hitter who had been ejected from three games in five days in 1913—and traded Fred Merkle to Brooklyn. Realizing that the great Christy Mathewson was finally at the end of the line, McGraw sent him to Cincinnati, where he would serve as manager, for pitcher John "Rube" Benton and infielder Buck Herzog. Ex–Federal League star Benny Kauff became an everyday outfielder. The upshot of all this was that in the second half, the Giants went on an alltime record 26-game home winning streak but still managed to come in fourth. In St. Louis, future Hall-of-Famer Rogers Hornsby played his first full season, batting .313, and in Chicago, dead-ball great Three

Finger Brown recorded his 239th and final career win against only 130 losses; his lifetime ERA of 2.06 is the third-lowest in 20th-century history.

In the AL, Boston lost Tris Speaker to Cleveland in a salary dispute but still repeated, finishing two games ahead of Chicago with a 91–63 record. Nineteen sixteen was almost the same story as 1915 for the Red Sox, as their mediocre hitters were carried by an awesome pitching staff that included emerging ace Babe Ruth, who won 23 games and the ERA title at 1.75, Dutch Leonard, Rube Foster, and underhand power pitcher Carl Mays. The Sox staff led the AL in shutouts with 24 and finished second in team ERA to a Chicago staff of Eddie Cicotte, ERA runner-up at 1.78; Urban "Red" Faber, who had an ERA of 2.02; Reb Russell; and young Claude "Lefty" Williams.

Ty Cobb's Tigers finished third, four games out, as Cobb led the AL in stolen bases and runs; for the first time since he had become a regular player in 1907, Cobb lost the batting title. He was beaten out by Tris Speaker, who outhit him .386 to .371 and led the league in hits with 211, doubles with 41, on-base average at .470 and slugging average at .502. Joe Jackson, traded before the season from Cleveland to the White Sox, hit .341, third-best in the AL, and hit 21 triples. The 1916 Series was a reprise of 1915, as Boston pitched its way past Brooklyn in five games.

CHAPTER NINE

A Corkscrew Mind: Hal Chase and the Corruption of Major-league Baseball

In a personal statement appended to his 1919 biography, *Commy*, AL co-founder and White Sox owner Charles Comiskey writes:

> [Baseball] is the most honest pastime in the world. It has to be or it could not last a season out. Crookedness and baseball do not mix. This year, 1919, is the greatest season of them all.[1]

Not only was this not true, but Comiskey knew that it was not true when he wrote it. In the 1910s, corruption was working its way through the major leagues like a cancer. Since its last corruption scandal in 1877, major-league baseball had progressed from an easy attitude toward gambling, to tolerating one team paying another a reward for "bearing down" against an opponent, to fixing the odd game, as long as it did not affect the pennant race. By the last years of the dead-ball era, there seemed to be no rules at all. Comiskey's White Sox were as badly infected as any team in baseball; as

Comiskey wrote these words, the White Sox were on their way to the AL pennant and first baseman Chick Gandil and seven teammates were conspiring to fix the outcome of the 1919 World Series in return for large bribes from gamblers. When the so-called Black Sox scandal broke a year later and the nation's fans discovered that even a sacred institution like the World Series might not be on the up-and-up, major-league baseball came very close to self-destruction.

When the story of the 1919 World Series is told, the players are usually portrayed as naive bumblers, trapped and manipulated by cynical gangsters and gamblers. The evidence suggests, however, that the players may well have been the cynical ones and that they recruited gamblers into their scheme, not the other way around. Certainly, the men behind the Black Sox affair and most of the other misdeeds of the late dead-ball era were savvy veterans, not innocent rookies. Comiskey and his fellow baseball owners behaved cynically as well. For years they had swept lesser scandals under the rug; the players had learned from experience that teammates who threw games, manipulated scores, or bet on baseball would go unpunished.

The Black Sox scandal was not an isolated incident; it was merely the last, and possibly the worst, in a long train of abuses. How far back did it go? In 1918, outfielder Lee Magee, who had been caught plotting with Hal Chase and Heinie Zimmerman to fix individual games, threatened to tell the world about "tricks turned since 1906." Even though he never made good on this threat, it does seem as though there was a steady increase in rumors of corruption starting around that time and reaching a crescendo in 1918–20.

THE YEAR: 1917

John McGraw's retooled New York Giants won the pennant in a laugher over Philadelphia, who faded after slumps by Luderus and George "Dode" Paskert, as well as newcomers Johnny Evers, who hit .224 and retired following the season, and Wildfire Schulte, who hit .214 in his second-to-last season. The Phillies would have finished much farther back if not for another stellar performance by Pete Alexander, who led the NL in wins with 30, complete games with 35, shutouts with 8, strikeouts with 201, innings pitched with 388, and ERA at 1.86.

McGraw's new-look offense of Heinie Zimmerman, who led the league in RBIs with 102; George Burns, the runs scored leader with 103; and Dave Robertson, who knocked an NL-high 12 home runs, produced a league-best 635 runs. New York pitchers led the NL in fewest runs allowed with 457. Lefty Ferdie Schupp went 21–7 to lead the NL in winning percentage at .750; Schupp was one of four New York starters to win more than 15 games.

Ex–Federal Leaguer Edd Roush of Cincinnati won the batting title at .341, beating out third-place St. Louis's Rogers Hornsby, who batted .327 and led the league in triples with 17. At Cincinnati, 24-win man Fred Toney hooked up with Chicago's James "Hippo" Vaughn for major league history's only double no-hitter. With one out in the tenth, Reds shortstop Larry Kopf singled for the first hit of the game and moved to third base on a fly ball misplayed by centerfielder Cy Williams; he scored the winning run on an infield dribbler by Olympic legend Jim Thorpe, who spent six frustrating years in the big leagues as the world's fastest .250 hitter. In Pittsburgh, Honus Wagner retired with a .329 lifetime batting average compiled in a 21-year career that coincided almost exactly with the dead-ball era. He joined a crowd of legends who retired in 1917, including Ed Walsh, Ed Reulbach, and Eddie Plank.

Charles Comiskey's burgeoning Chicago White Sox dynasty took the AL pennant, going 100–54 with a lineup, and a set of morale problems, virtually identical to that of the infamous 1919 squad: the evil Charles "Chick" Gandil at first, squeaky clean Eddie Collins at second, Charles "Swede" Risberg at short, Buck Weaver at third, Ray Schalk behind the plate, and Oscar "Happy" Felsch and Joe Jackson in the outfield. Felsch hit .308, fifth in the league, and Jackson hit .301 with 17 triples. Once again, Boston led the league in pitching thanks to Carl Mays, second in the AL in ERA at 1.74; Babe Ruth, second in wins with 24; and Ernie Shore, but the Red Sox could not match the White Sox's hitting. Ty Cobb staged something of a comeback, winning the batting title at .383, hitting 30 points better than St. Louis's George Sisler, as well as leading in stolen bases with 55, hits with 225, doubles with 44, and triples with 23.

Chicago won the World Series 4–2, as the Giants suffered one of their patented postseason collapses in the fourth inning of game six. Heinie Zimmerman's throwing error put Eddie Collins on second; then, Dave Robertson dropped Joe Jackson's harmless fly to right. With runners on first and third, pitcher Rube Benton fielded Happy Felsch's come-backer and caught Collins too far off third. He threw to Zimmerman, who vainly chased Collins toward home plate, which both first baseman Holke and catcher Rariden had neglected to cover.

At an organizational meeting the day before the opening game of the 1907 World Series between Detroit and Chicago, players representative Herman "Germany" Schaefer, who was also the Tigers' second baseman, had asked National Commission chairman Garry Herrmann if a tie counted as a legal game. When Herrmann asked what difference it made, Schaefer explained that under the rules, the players shared in the profits from the first four legal series games only. (This was designed to prevent corruption by giving players no financial incentive for dragging out the series to the maximum number of games.) The commission then ruled that if there was a tie, the players would share in the gate from the first five games. That same afternoon, the Tigers and Cubs played—you guessed it—a very strange-looking, error-filled 12-inning tie that was marred by dropped third strikes, uncontested stolen bases, and a bizarre interference call that prevented the winning run from scoring for Chicago in the tenth. In response to widespread public doubts about the game's honesty, Ban Johnson had the matter investigated. He found no evidence of corruption.

Rumors of corruption circled around a series between the Phillies and Giants during the 1908 pennant race. After the Black Sox scandal exploded 12 years later, catcher Charles "Red" Dooin of the Phillies confirmed that members of the New York Giants had offered him and several teammates an immense sum of money to throw a series of regular season games. In 1910 there was the Chalmers award scandal involving Lajoie and Cobb. In 1911, when a young sportswriter named Fred Lieb arrived in New York to work for the *New York Press*, he found that "there was talk of crookedness in baseball but no effort was being made to pin anything down on anyone." Much of the talk centered on Yankees first baseman Hal Chase, about whom Lieb's editor Jim Price gave this scouting report: "He is a remarkable fielder. I don't think anyone ever played first base as well as Hal Chase can play it—if he wants to play it. But he has a corkscrew brain."[2]

In 1916, during a season-ending series between Wilbert Robinson's Brooklyn Dodgers and John McGraw's Giants, manager McGraw suddenly stormed off the bench in anger and accused his players of "quitting." The Dodgers, a team loaded with ex-Giants, won both games and edged out Philadelphia for the NL pennant. The *New York Times* commented that "it would

151

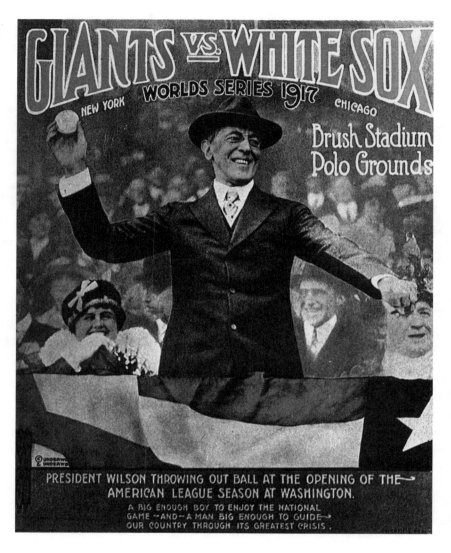

The cover of the 1917 World Series program
shows President Woodrow Wilson throwing out
the first pitch at the Washington Senators'
Opening Day ceremonies.

take no mind reader to understand that when it came to a question of the pennant going to Philadelphia or Brooklyn, just where the New York players would rest."[3] McGraw later claimed that he had only become angry because the Giants were "disregarding his signals."

THE YEAR: 1918

In 1918, baseball entered World War I. War had been formally declared in April 1917, but players did not begin to join the armed services in significant numbers until Provost Marshall Crowder, the government official who supervised the military draft, issued his "work or fight" order in June 1918. Baseball made no attempt to claim essential employment status on the grounds that it aided public morale, as it would do during World War II, and the government ordered the season cut short on Labor Day, September 2. Roughly half of all major leaguers signed up or were drafted, and personnel losses were a determining factor in both pennant races.

In the AL, the defending champion White Sox lost Red Faber, Swede Risberg, Joe Jackson, Happy Felsch, and Lefty Williams; they dropped to sixth place, 17 games out. A depleted Cleveland Indians team finished second, only 2½ games behind, thanks to big hitting seasons from Tris Speaker and shortstop Ray Chapman. The pennant winner was a completely overhauled Boston Red Sox team that was run by executive Ed Barrow after manager Jack Barry was drafted. Barrow filled the holes in his line-up by borrowing Stuffy McInnis, Wally Schang, and Joe Bush from the last-place Athletics and altered the course of history by playing staff ace Babe Ruth in the outfield, mostly against righties, between starts. The Babe went 13–7 with a 2.22 ERA on the mound, but batted .300 with 11 triples and 66 RBIs—fourth-best in the AL—in only 317 times at bat.

He won the first of 12 career home run titles with 11 homers. The 31-year-old Ty Cobb won the 1918 batting title at .382 and led in triples with 14. Walter Johnson won 23 games, most in the league, and the ERA title at 1.27.

The draft cost the defending champion Giants outfielder Benny Kauff, pitcher Rube Benton, and pitcher Jeff Tesreau; McGraw's team finished second, 10½ games behind Chicago. The relatively intact Cubs turned the pennant race into a cakewalk on the strength of Fred Merkle's .297 batting average and 65 RBIs and Hippo Vaughn's league-leading 22 wins and 1.74 ERA. Brooklyn's Zach Wheat won the batting title at .335, barely nosing out Edd Roush, who hit .333. The third-place Reds suspended first baseman Hal Chase 74 games into the season for "indifferent play."

The 1918 season ended on another ugly note, when both teams refused to take the field for game one of the World Series after learning that they would be receiving less than their promised share of the take. The players were finally forced to give in after an appeal to their patriotism by Ban Johnson; the owners managed to ignore the players' compromise proposal that all proceeds be donated to a war charity. The 1918 series saw the first playing of the national anthem before a baseball game; it proved so popular that it was soon extended to all World Series games and then to the rest of the season.

There are far too many rumored, alleged, or confessed instances of game fixing and bribery in 1918 and 1919 to list here. The explosion of rumors about fixed games was so striking that many in baseball wondered if the government's closing of horse racing tracks for the duration of the war might have something to do with it. A fairly large percentage of these incidents, however, have something else in common: the involvement of

Hal Chase or one or more of his accomplices—pitcher Rube Benton, third baseman Heinie Zimmerman, utility man Lee Magee, outfielder Benny Kauff, and pitcher Jean Dubuc.

Who was Hal Chase? Born near Los Angeles, the right-handed hitting, left-handed fielding Chase became an instant star in 1905, his first year with the New York Highlanders, as the Yankees were then known. A good line-drive hitter, Chase was the Keith Hernandez of the dead-ball era; he was such an amazing fielder that people who saw him never got over it. "In agility and quickness of movement, Chase was in a class by himself," remembered Ed Barrow, "As a fielding first baseman he was unmatched and without a doubt whatsoever the greatest who ever lived." Both Walter Johnson and Lou Gehrig's teammate Babe Ruth named Chase as the first baseman on their all-time greatest teams. As sportswriter Fred Lieb soon noticed, however, appearance and reality did not always coincide with Hal Chase. "I looked up Chase's fielding averages and discovered that for about six years in succession, Chase, supposedly the peerless first baseman, wound up with 19 to 21 errors. Now that, I knew, was pretty unusual for a first baseman."[4] One day in 1913, Yankees manager Frank Chance came up to Lieb and complained about several good throws from infielders that Chase had muffed. "He's throwing games on me!" Chance blurted out. A few days after Lieb printed Chance's remark, Chase was traded to the White Sox.

This was not the first problem with the manager-killing Chase. In 1908 he had been accused by manager Clark Griffith of "laying down." In 1910 new Yankees manager George Stallings confronted Chase about some suspicious plays. Chase's response was to go to Yankees owner Frank Farrell; Farrell fired Stallings and replaced him with Chase. Ban Johnson scolded Stallings for "besmirch[ing] the character of a sterling player," and stated, "anybody who knows Hal Chase knows that he is not guilty of the accusations." As Highlanders third baseman Jimmy Austin recalled in *The Glory of Their Times,* "Well, you know how good a manager Hal Chase was: so good that he took over a club that finished second in 1910 and took them straight to sixth place in 1911. And the year after that they wound up last." Frank Chance was given the job in 1913.

After the Federal League folded, Chase ended up in Cincinnati under manager Christy Mathewson. In August 1918, Matty suspended Chase and brought him up before NL president John Heydler on charges of throwing games. By the time the charges were heard, however, Mathewson was with the army in France and most of his witnesses were unavailable. Chase was acquitted after John McGraw, Mathewson's best friend, testified to Chase's good character. The Giants manager then signed both Chase and Heinie Zimmerman for the 1919 season. Finally, after Chase had spent the better part of thirteen years dropping throws from his infielders, failing to cover first base, and bribing and corrupting as many of his fellow major leaguers as possible, the NL banned Chase for life in late 1919. He remains the holder of the AL record for most career errors at first base, 279.

After playing a behind-the-scenes role in the plot to throw the 1919 World Series, Hal Chase returned to the West, playing in outlaw leagues in California, Arizona, and New Mexico. After a few years he wrote to Commissioner Landis, admitted that he had made "mistakes," and begged for reinstatement. Landis answered by telling Chase that he was unaware that Chase had done anything wrong and just what were these mistakes? Landis never got a reply. Lost in a world of poker games, pool hustling, and alcoholism—and banned for life from setting foot in any California minor-league park—Hal Chase died penniless at 64 of a vitamin deficiency caused by his drinking.

In a sort of deathbed confession, Chase told a reporter that he had gotten involved with gamblers because he "wasn't satisfied with what the club owners paid me. Like others, I had to have a bet on the side and we used to bet with the other team and the gamblers who sat in the boxes. . . . Once the evil started there was no stopping it and club owners were not strong enough to cope with the evil." Hal Chase was probably a psychopath, someone who lacks a basic understanding of right and wrong. As one friend from his outlaw-league days put it, "[Chase] was completely and congenitally amoral." Like many psychopaths, Chase was superficially charming and intelligent, but lacking in insight and ultimately self-defeating; he handled his inevitable failures by shifting the responsibility to someone else.

THE YEAR: 1919

Baseball returned to business as usual when the war ended in 1919. For eight members of the best team in baseball, the Chicago White Sox, that meant finding a way to sell the 1919 World Series to the highest bidder. The Sox' opponent proved to be a surprising Cincinnati Reds team led by hitters Edd Roush, Heinie Groh, Jake Daubert, and little lead-off man Morrie Rath. The Reds staff of Harry "Slim" Sallee, Hod Eller, and Walter "Dutch" Ruether allowed the fewest runs in the league. Cincinnati ran away with the NL flag, finishing 9 games ahead of the Giants.

The powerful Sox had a surprisingly difficult time of it in the AL race. Chicago came in 3½ games ahead of Cleveland but lost a number of suspicious-looking games down the stretch in what may have been a warm-up for the greatest betrayal of public trust in base-

WHEN GAMBLING CONTROLLED

*This cartoon, entitled "When Gambling Controlled,"
depicts gambling's effect on baseball. The 1919
Black Sox scandal undermined public confidence in
the game and nearly destroyed major-league baseball.*

ball history. The White Sox had Joe Jackson's power,
Eddie Collins's speed, and a fearsome starting four of
shine-ball artist Eddie Cicotte, Lefty Williams, Dickie
Kerr, and Red Faber. Boston finished out of the money

in sixth place but caused a sensation when converted pitcher Babe Ruth hit .322 with an AL-high 114 RBIs and an all-time record 29 homers, including four grand slams. Detroit's Ty Cobb won his final batting title, hitting .384.

The underdog Reds became only the second NL club to win the World Series in the decade of the 1910s, when the White Sox deliberately lost the best-of-nine series, five games to three. Many sportswriters, including Hugh Fullerton and Ring Lardner, smelled a rat—during the series, Lardner waltzed through the White Sox' train car singing the following lyrics to the tune of "I'm Forever Blowing Bubbles":

> *I'm forever blowing ball games,*
> *Pretty ball games in the air.*
> *I come from Chi*
> *I hardly try*
> *Just go to bat and fade and die;*
> *Fortune's coming my way,*
> *That's why I don't care.*
> *I'm forever blowing ball games,*
> *and the gamblers treat us fair. . . .*

Reportedly, there was no reaction from the Chicago players. As the public learned almost one year later when the scandal broke, the most exciting moments in the 1919 series came in games three and six, when the honest Dickie Kerr won 3-0 and 5-4, while several of his teammates were doing their best to lose.

Fred Lieb felt that the example of the popular Hal Chase, and his apparent untouchability, inspired many younger major leaguers to go bad. "How many good young ballplayers," Lieb wrote, "may have said, 'Chase gets by with it, year after year, so why shouldn't we pick up a little extra money when the chance is offered us?'

159

And how many, when tempted, fell?"[5] But there are always Hal Chases. The real tragedy of the 1910s was as much the irresponsibility of the men who ran the game as the corruptibility of their players. Not only did the owners do a poor job of policing baseball, their own greed created an atmosphere that encouraged corruption. Throughout the peace of 1903–14, the lords of baseball were making money hand over fist and giving as little of it as possible to the players. Then the Federal League War drove up salaries by two or three times, showing players what they were worth in an open market. When the FL war was settled and player salaries were immediately cut back to 1900s levels, the players—especially veteran players and stars—resented it bitterly.

Second, as the story of Hal Chase shows, the owners were content to ignore evidence of corruption, even if three of the most respected men in baseball—George Stallings, Frank Chance, and Christy Mathewson—brought it to their attention. One reason for this was a cynical instinct to sweep all bad news under the rug; another may have been the fact that the baseball owners were far from moral paragons themselves. Baseball National Commission members Ban Johnson and Garry Herrmann were both known to place the occasional bet on a baseball game. In 1906 Herrmann was very embarrassed when it got out that he had bet a trio of professional gamblers $6,000 that Pittsburgh would not win the pennant. The New York Giants and other teams were very hospitable to gamblers and bookmakers, who enjoyed their own special facilities in many major-league parks. John McGraw even went into business with underworld fixer Arnold Rothstein; Rothstein later arranged for an associate, Charles Stoneham, to buy the Giants. This is the same Arnold Rothstein who was indicted for bankrolling the 1919 World Series fix.

When Frank Chance complained to Yankees owner Frank Farrell about Hal Chase's involvement with gamblers, he was complaining to one of the biggest bookmakers and gamblers in New York City.

The story of Lee Magee's trade to the Chicago Cubs tells us a lot about the 1910s, because it shows how many feathers were ruffled when a baseball owner did try to do the right thing. Magee, a partner-in-crime of Hal Chase's, was traded in the middle of 1919 from Brooklyn to the Cubs. During the off-season, new Cubs owner Albert Lasker released Magee and refused to pay the guaranteed year that was left on his contract. The reason for this was that Lasker, an advertising man with no baseball experience other than the years he had spent as a fan going to nearly every Cubs home game, had been shocked to discover that Magee was throwing games. Magee took the Cubs to court, demanding his money and threatening to expose four other corrupt players if he did not get it. Lasker got a second shock when he discovered that his fellow owners knew all about Magee's activities but did not care; to a man, they urged him to pay Magee off and avoid a trial that might damage baseball's reputation.

It was this episode that inspired Albert Lasker to devote himself to cleaning up the major leagues. Even though he started out with little influence in the world of baseball, Lasker was active in Chicago politics and well connected in national Republican circles. Within a year he had put forth the so-called Lasker plan. More or less laughed off by Ban Johnson and his fellow baseball magnates, the plan called for baseball to be cleaned up and permanently governed by a panel of distinguished and disinterested outsiders, men like fellow Republicans General John J. Pershing, Senator Hiram Johnson, and a whitehaired federal judge whom Lasker often ran into at Cubs games—Kenesaw Mountain Landis.

161

SOURCE NOTES

CHAPTER ONE
1. Albert Spalding, *America's National Game* (San Francisco: Halo Books, 1991), p. 191.
2. Eugene Murdock, *Ban Johnson, Czar of Baseball* (Westport, CT: Greenwood Press, 1982), p. 24.

CHAPTER TWO
1. Bill James, *The Bill James Historical Baseball Abstract* (New York: Villard Books, 1988), p. 58.

CHAPTER THREE
1. Lawrence Ritter, *The Glory of Their Times* (New York: William Morrow and Co., 1984), p. 176.
2. Gerald Astor, ed., *The Baseball Hall of Fame 50th Anniversary Book* (New York: Prentice Hall, 1988), p. 74.
3. Christy Mathewson, *Pitching in a Pinch* (New York: Grosset and Dunlap, 1912), pp. 54–55.
4. Gerald Astor, ed., *The Baseball Hall of Fame 50th Anniversary Book* (New York: Prentice Hall, 1988), p. 56.

CHAPTER FOUR
1. G. H. Fleming, in *The National Pastime #1,* vol. I (Cooperstown, NY: S.A.B.R., 1982), p. 29.
2. G. H. Fleming, *The Unforgettable Season* (New York: Penguin Books, 1981), p. 248.
3. G. H. Fleming, in *The National Pastime #1,* vol. I (Cooperstown, NY: S.A.B.R., 1982), p. 30.
4. G. H. Fleming, *The Unforgettable Season* (New York: Penguin Books, 1981), p. 247.

5. Lee Allen, *The National League Story* (New York: Hill and Wang, 1961), p. 118.

CHAPTER FIVE
1. Ed Barrow, *My Fifty Years in Baseball* (New York: Coward McCann, 1951), p. 33.
2. Craig Wright and Tom House, *The Diamond Appraised* (New York: Simon and Schuster, 1989), p. 366.

CHAPTER SIX
1. Fred Lieb, *The Story of the World Series* (New York: G. P. Putnam's Sons, 1965), p. 83.
2. A. D. Suehsdorf, in *The National Pastime, #2, vol. IV* (Cooperstown, NY: S.A.B.R., 1985), p. 37.
3. Lawrence Ritter, *The Glory of Their Times* (New York: William Morrow and Co., 1984), pp. 26–27.

CHAPTER SEVEN
1. Michael Gershman, *Diamonds* (Boston: Houghton Mifflin, 1993), p. 83.

CHAPTER EIGHT
1. Ernie Lanigan, *The Baseball Cyclopedia* (New York: The Baseball Magazine Co., 1922), p. 10.

CHAPTER NINE
1. G. W. Axelson, *Commy* (Chicago: Reilly and Lee, 1919), p. 318.
2. Fred Lieb, *Baseball As I Have Known It* (New York: Grosset and Dunlap, 1977), p. 105.
3. Harold Seymour, *Baseball, The Golden Age* (New York: Oxford Univ. Press, 1971), p. 287.
4. Fred Lieb, *Baseball As I Have Known It* (New York: Grosset and Dunlap, 1977), p. 106.
5. Fred Lieb, *Baseball As I Have Known It* (New York: Grosset and Dunlap, 1977), p. 113.

Bibliography

Alexander, Charles. *John McGraw*. New York: Viking, 1988.

———. *Ty Cobb*. New York: Oxford Univ. Press, 1984.

Allen, Lee. *100 Years of Baseball*. New York: Bartholomew House, 1950.

———. *The American League Story*. New York: Hill and Wang, 1962.

———. *The National League Story*. New York: Hill and Wang, 1961.

Axelson, G. W. *Commy*. Chicago: Reilly and Lee, 1919.

Cobb, Ty, with Al Stump. *My Life in Baseball—The True Record*. Garden City, NY: Doubleday and Co., 1961.

Fleming, G. H. *The Unforgettable Season*. New York: Penguin Books, 1981.

Gershman, Michael. *Diamonds: The Evolution of the Ballpark*. Boston: Houghton Mifflin Co., 1993.

James, Bill. *The Bill James Historical Baseball Abstract*. New York: Villard Books, 1988.

Lieb, Fred. *Baseball As I Have Known It*. New York: Grosset and Dunlap, 1977.

———. *The Story of the World Series*. New York: G. P. Putnam's Sons, 1965.

Mathewson, Christy. *Pitching in a Pinch*. New York: Grosset and Dunlap, 1912.

Murdock, Eugene. *Ban Johnson, Czar of Baseball*. Westport, CT: Greenwood Press, 1982.

Okkonen, Marc. *The Federal League of 1914–1915.*
    Garret Park, MD: S.A.B.R., 1989.
Quigley, Martin. *The Crooked Pitch.* Chapel Hill:
    Algonquin Books, 1984.
Reichler, Joseph, ed. *The Baseball Encyclopedia.* New
    York: Macmillan Pub. Co., 1988.
Ritter, Lawrence. *The Glory of Their Times.* New York:
    William Morrow and Co., 1984.
Seymour, Harold. *Baseball: The Golden Age.* New York:
    Oxford Univ. Press, 1971.
Thorn, John and Palmer, Pete, eds. *Total Baseball,* 3rd
    ed. New York: HarperCollins, 1993.

MAJOR LEAGUES, TEAMS, AND CITIES (1871–1957)

League Name (Years of existence): City Name (Years in league)

NATIONAL ASSOCIATION (1871–75):
Boston (1871–75), Philadelphia (1871–75),[1] Chicago (1871, 1874–75), Washington (1871–73, 1875),[2] Troy, NY (1871–72), New York City (1871–75), Cleveland (1871–72), Ft. Wayne, IN (1871), Baltimore (1872–74)[3], Brooklyn (1872–75),[4] Rockford, IL (1871), Middletown, CT (1872), Elizabeth, NJ (1873), Hartford, CT (1874–75), St. Louis (1875),[5] New Haven, CT (1875), Keokuk, IA (1875).

[1] two franchises (1873–74); three franchises (1875)
[2] two franchises (1872)
[3] two franchises (1873)
[4] two franchises (1872)
[5] two franchises (1875)

NATIONAL LEAGUE (1876–Present):
Chicago (1876–Present), St. Louis (1876–77, 1885–86,

1892–Present), Hartford, CT (1876–77), Boston (1876–1952), Louisville, KY (1876–77, 1892–99), New York City (1876, 1883–1957), Philadelphia (1876, 1883–Present), Cincinnati (1876–80, 1890–Present), Providence, RI (1878–85), Indianapolis (1878, 1887–89), Milwaukee (1878, 1953–65), Buffalo (1879–85), Cleveland (1879–84, 1889–99), Syracuse, NY (1879), Troy, NY (1879–82), Worcester, MA (1880–82), Detroit (1881–88), Kansas City (1886), Washington, DC (1886–89, 1892–99), Pittsburgh (1887–Present), Brooklyn (1890–1957), Baltimore (1892–99)

AMERICAN ASSOCIATION (1882–1891):
Cincinnati (1882–89, 1891), Philadelphia (1882–91), Louisville, KY (1882–1891), Pittsburgh (1882–1886), St. Louis (1882–91), Baltimore (1882–91), Boston (1891), Brooklyn (1884–90), Cleveland (1887–88), Columbus, OH (1883–84, 1889–91), Indianapolis (1884), Kansas City (1888–89), Milwaukee (1891), New York City (1883–87), Richmond, VA (1884), Rochester, NY (1890), Toledo, OH (1884, 1890), Washington, DC (1884, 1891)

UNION ASSOCIATION (1884):
Altoona, PA, Baltimore, Boston, Chicago, Cincinnati, Kansas City, Milwaukee, Philadelphia, Pittsburgh, St. Louis, St. Paul, MN, Washington, DC, Wilmington, DE

PLAYERS LEAGUE (1890):
Boston, Brooklyn, Buffalo, Chicago, Cleveland, New York City, Philadelphia, Pittsburgh

AMERICAN LEAGUE (1901–Present):
Baltimore (1901–02, 1954–Present), Boston (1901–Present), Chicago (1901–Present), Cleveland

(1901–Present), Detroit (1901–Present), Kansas City (1955–67), Milwaukee (1901), New York City (1903–Present), Philadelphia (1901–54), St. Louis (1902–53), Washington, DC (1901–71)

FEDERAL LEAGUE (1914–15):
Baltimore (1914–15), Brooklyn (1914–15), Indianapolis (1914), Chicago (1914–15), Buffalo (1914–15), Kansas City (1914–15), Pittsburgh (1914–15), St. Louis (1914–15), Newark, NJ (1915)

APPENDIX B

INDEX OF MAJOR-LEAGUE CITIES AND TEAM NAMES (1871–1957)

City: League[1] (Years in league), Nickname(s)[2]

ALTOONA, PA: UA (1884)

BALTIMORE: NA (1872–74) Lord Baltimores; NA (1873) Marylands; AA (1882–91) Orioles; UA (1884); NL (1892–99) Orioles; AL (1901–02) *Orioles (ancestor of today's New York Yankees)*; AL (1954–Present) *Orioles*; FL (1914–15) Terrapins

BOSTON: NA (1871–75) Red Stockings; NL (1876–1952) Red Stockings, Beaneaters, *Braves (ancestor of today's Atlanta Braves)*; UA (1884); PL (1890) Red Stockings; AA (1891); AL (1901–Present) Puritans, Pilgrims, Somersets, *Red Sox*

BROOKLYN: NA (1872–75) Atlantics; NA (1872) Eckfords; AA (1884–90) Gladiators, Grays, Bridegrooms; PL (1890) Wonders; NL (1890–1957) Superbas, Robins, *Dodgers (ancestor of today's Los Angeles Dodgers)*; FL (1914–15) Tip-Tops

BUFFALO: NL (1879–85) Bisons; PL (1890) Bisons; FL (1914–15) Blues

CHICAGO: NA (1871, 1874–75) White Stockings; NL (1876–Present) White Stockings, Colts, Orphans, *Cubs*; UA (1884) Browns; PL (1890) Pirates; AL (1901–Present) *White Sox*; FL (1914–15) Whales

CINCINNATI: NL (1876–80, 1890–Present) Red Stockings, Redlegs, *Reds*; AA 1882–89, 1891) Red Stockings, Porkers; UA (1884) Outlaw Reds

CLEVELAND: NA (1871–72) Forest Citys; NL (1879–84, 1889–99) Blues; AA (1887–88) Spiders; PL (1890) Infants; AL (1901–Present) Blues, Bronchos, Naps, *Indians*

COLUMBUS, OH: AA (1883–84, 1889–91) Colts, Senators, Solons

DETROIT: NL (1881–88) Wolverines; AL (1901–Present) *Tigers*

ELIZABETH, NJ: NA (1873) Resolutes

FT. WAYNE, IN: NA (1871) Kekiongas

HARTFORD, CT: NA (1874–75) Dark Blues; NL (1876–77)

INDIANAPOLIS: NL (1878, 1887-89) Hoosiers, Browns; AA (1884) Blues; FL (1914) Hoosiers

KANSAS CITY: UA (1884); NL (1886) Cowboys; AA (1888–89) Blues; UA (1884); FL (1914–15) Packers; AL (1955–67) *Athletics (ancestor of today's Oakland Athletics)*

KEOKUK, IA: NA (1875) Westerns

LOUISVILLE, KY: NL (1876–77, 1892-99) Grays; AA (1882–91) Eclipse, Colonels, Cyclones

MIDDLETOWN, CT: NA (1872) Mansfields

MILWAUKEE: NL (1878) Grays, Cream Citys; UA (1884) Grays; AA (1891) Brewers; NL (1953–65) *Braves (ancestor of today's Atlanta Braves)*; AL (1901) Brewers

NEWARK, NJ: FL (1915) Peppers

NEW HAVEN, CT: NA (1875) Elm Citys

NEW YORK CITY: NA (1871–75) Mutuals; NL (1876) Mutuals; NL (1883–1957) Gothams, *Giants (ancestor of today's San Francisco Giants)*; AA (1883–87) Metropolitans; PL (1890) Giants; AL (1903–Present) Highlanders, Hilltoppers, *Yankees*

PHILADELPHIA: NA (1871–75) Athletics; NA (1873–75) White Stockings, Pearls, Philadelphias; NA (1875) Centennials; NL (1876, 1883–Present) Athletics, Blue Jays, *Phillies*; AA (1882–91) Athletics; UA (1884) Keystones; PL (1890) Quakers; AL (1901–54) *Athletics, A's (ancestor of today's Oakland Athletics)*

PITTSBURGH: AA (1882–86) Alleghenys; UA (1884) Stogies; NL (1887–Present) Alleghenys, *Pirates*; PL (1890) Burghers, Innocents; FL (1914-15) Rebels, Stogies

PROVIDENCE: NL (1878–85) Grays

RICHMOND, VA: AA (1884) Virginias

ROCKFORD, IL: NA (1871) Forest Citys

ROCHESTER, NY: AA (1890)

ST. LOUIS: NA (1875) Red Stockings; NA (1875) Brown Stockings; NL (1876–77, 1885–86, 1892–Present) Brown Stockings, Browns, Perfectos, *Cardinals*; AA (1882–91) Browns; UA (1884) Maroons; AL (1902–53) *Browns (ancestor of today's Baltimore Orioles)*; FL (1914–15) Terriers

ST. PAUL, MN: UA (1884) White Caps

SYRACUSE, NY: NL (1879) Stars; AA (1890) Stars

TOLEDO, OH: AA (1884, 1890) Blue Stockings, Maumees

TROY, NY: NA (1871–72) Unions, Haymakers; NL (1879–82) Trojans

WASHINGTON, DC: NA (1871–72) Olympics; NA (1872–73, 1875) Nationals; AA (1884, 1891) Nationals, Senators; UA (1884) Nationals; NL (1886–89, 1892–99) Senators; AL (1901–71) *Senators (ancestor of today's Texas Rangers)*

WILMINGTON, DE: UA (1884)

WORCESTER, MA: NL (1880–82) Brown Stockings

[1] League abbreviations: NA = National Association, NL = National League, AA = American Association, UA = Union Association, PL = Players League, AL = American League, FL = Federal League
[2] Only more common nicknames given; nickname not provided for every team/league/year. NB: Clubs from same city in different year or different league are not necessarily related.

NB: Italics = same as contemporary franchise or ancestor of contemporary franchise

INDEX

African-American baseball, 19, 102, 104–105
Alexander, Grover Cleveland "Pete," 55, 105, 116, 140, 145, 149
American Association, 9, 10, 11, 19, 22
American League, 18, 23, 24, 25, 26, 35, 42, 44, 59, 92
Anson, Adrian "Cap," 9, 23, 34, 58, 125, 138

Baker, Frank "Home Run," 93, 97, 106, 108, 116, 124, 128
Ballparks, 127–28, 131–33
Baltimore Orioles, 11, 13, 31, 49, 70, 101, 108, 110, 111, 144
Barrow, Ed, 87, 88, 89, 119, 120, 153, 155
Black Sox scandal, 40, 60, 148, 151, 159
Boston Beaneaters, 11, 41, 111, 117
Boston Braves, 58, 100, 111, 124, 131, 136, 140

Boston Red Sox, 23, 25, 27, 35, 37–43, 47–50, 58, 87, 93, 100, 109, 117–20, 124, 126, 136, 139–40, 144, 148, 150, 153, 158
Brooklyn Dodgers, 13, 76, 110, 128, 129, 131, 133, 145, 151
Brown, Mordecai "Three Finger," 64, 66, 67, 73, 76, 84, 105, 107, 112–14, 123, 146
Brush, John, 19, 20, 32, 43, 48, 52, 101

Chadwick, Henry, 34, 77–78
Chance, Frank, 51, 65, 66, 71, 78, 80, 84, 106, 112, 114, 124, 155, 156, 160
Chase, Hal, 63, 136, 139, 148, 151, 154, 155–57, 159, 160, 161
Chesbro, Jack, 26, 29, 33, 42, 44–50, 51, 52–54, 55, 86

173

Chicago Cubs, 23, 25, 51, 60, 64, 65–66, 67, 71, 72, 75, 78, 79, 80–81, 82, 83, 92, 100, 106–7, 111, 114, 124, 131, 139, 140, 141, 144, 149, 151, 154, 161

Chicago White Sox, 23, 25, 43, 58, 59, 66, 67, 74, 75, 76, 110, 124, 130, 139, 146, 147–48, 149–50, 153, 155, 159 *See also* Black Sox scandal

Cincinnati Reds, 19, 20, 32, 100, 115, 136, 154, 156, 159

Clarke, Fred, 26, 36, 89, 92, 101, 117

Cleveland Indians, 43, 50, 59, 66, 74, 75, 76, 94, 100, 116, 129, 146, 153, 157

Cobb, Ty, 58, 60, 68, 70, 71, 72, 73, 74, 87, 88, 91–92, 93, 94–99, 106, *107,* 116, 120, 121, 129, *130,* 136, 141, 146, 150, 151, 154, 159

Collins, Eddie, 93, 106, 110, 123, 129, 137, 150, 158

Collins, Jimmy, 11, 25, 26, 40, 41, 43, 117

Comiskey, Charles, 18, 19, 20, 21, 23, 24, 124, 147, 148, 149

Crawford, Wahoo Sam, 26, 60, 71, 76, 116, 129, *130,* 141

Delahanty, Big Ed, 12, 28, 32, 36, 58

Detroit Tigers, 70–71, 72, 74, 75, 76, 87, 91, 93, 98, 105, 114, 116, 129, 140, 141, 150, 151

Evers, Johnny, 51, 66, 73, 80, 83, 112, *113,* 116, 124, 137, 149

Federal League, 124, 131, 134–39, 143–45, 156, 160

Gambling, 15, 35, 39–40, 46, 62, 63, 147, 151, 154–56, *158,* 159–61

Griffith, Clark, 25, 30, 31, 35, 42, 44, 47, 48, 52, 54, 155

Hanlon, Ned, 11, 12, 13, 17, 102, 110, 111, 135, 145

Hooper, Harry, 109, 119, 140

Jackson, "Shoeless" Joe, 116, 129, *130,* 146, 150, 153, 158

Johnson, Ban, 18–19, 20, 21, 23, 24, 25, 27, 29, 30, 32, 34, 35, 42, 46, 48, 98, 101, 104, 106, 121, 126, 135, 151, 154, 160, 161

Johnson, Walter, 34, 55, 56, 57, 67–70, 71, 86, 105,

120–21, 129, 136, 141, 154

Joss, Adrian "Addie," 51, 74, 75, 86, 116

Keeler, Wee Willie, 11, 12, 13, 42, 43, 58, 59

Lajoie, Napoleon, 25, 26–27, 28, 35, 50, 58, 59, 67, 73, 88, 98, 106, *107,* 138, 151

Landis, Judge Kenesaw Mountain, 139, 143, 144, 161

Leach, Tommy, 29, 36, 92, 117, 118

McGillicuddy, Cornelius. *See* Connie Mack

McGinnity, Joe, 13, 14, 26, 30, 36, 51, 60, 78, 80, 101

McGraw, John, 9, 11, 25, 29–30, 36, 43, 48, 51, 58, 60, 63, 73, 78, 79, 81, 82, 84, 87, 100–5, 107, 109–10, 111, 114, 116, 121, *122,* 123, 125, 128, 136, 145, 148, 151, 153, 156, 160

Mack, Connie, 22, 25, 28, 74, 92, 100, 102, 106, 108, 109, 110, 116, 120–25, 128, 137

Marquard, Richard "Rube," 76, 104, 108, 115, 120, 124, 129, 130

Mathewson, Christy, 12, 26, 36, 51, 55, 56, 60–65,

73, 75, 78, 79, 81, 84, 86, 92, 101, 105, 108, 115, 120, 124, 129, 130–31, 137, 145, 156, 160

Merkle, Fred, 53, 78, 79, 80, 81, 82, 83–85, 104, 108, 109, 115, 120, 129, 145, 154

National Agreement, 21, 23, 32, 35

National League, 7, 8, 9, 10, 11, 12, 13, 14, 17, 18, 21, 23, 26, 29, 34, 35, 57, 93, 141

New York Giants, 15, 30, 31, 36, 43, 46, 48, 51, 60, 63, 64, 66, 70, 72, 76, 78, 79, 80, 83, 100, 101–5, 107–10, 114, 115, 116, 120, 121, 126, 128, 130, 136, 140, 143, 145, 148, 150, 151, 153, 154, 160

New York Highlanders, 31, 33, 35, 155

New York Yankees, 31, 35, 37–44, 46–50, 53, 66, 75, 100, 106, 119, 124, 133, 151, 155, 159, 161

Philadelphia Athletics, 23, 25, 27, 35, 43, 59, 60, 66, 71, 74, 92, 98, 100, 102, 107, 108, 109, 110, 114, 116, 121–25, 126,

127–28, 129, 130, 136, 137, 153

Philadelphia Phillies, 25, 27, 28, 100, 116, 139–40, 145, 148–49

Pittsburgh Pirates, 26, 33, 36, 39, 41, 44, 47, 51, 60, 71, 76, 78, 79, 81, 82, 86, 88, 89, 91, 92, 94, 101, 116, 117, 118, 131, 138, 160

Plank, Eddie, 35, 55, 59, 106, 123, 124, 130, 136, 149

Players League, 9, 10, 140, 143

Reserve clause, 10, 25, 30, 135, 138–39

Robinson, Wilbert, 11, 26, 110, 145, 151

Ruth, George "Babe," 29, 31, 34, 87–88, 96, 99, 119, 120, 132, 141, *142,* 144, 146, 150, 153–54, 159

St. Louis Browns, 9, 28, 74, 76, 100, 106, 144, 150

St. Louis Cardinals, 25, 28, 100, 117, 144

Selee, Frank, 11, 13, 111–12, 114, 117

Snodgrass, Fred, 53, 104, 108, 109, 115, 119, 130

Spalding, Albert, 15, *16,* 17, 18, 72, 141

Speaker, Tris, 119, 121, 146, 153

Tinker, Joe, 51, 65, 84, 112, 124, 136

Waddell, George "Rube," 12, 14, 35, 44, 51, 58, 59, 71, 74, 76, 86, 94, 123, 137

Wagner, John "Honus," 14, 26, 29, 33, 36, 39, 51, 58, 71, 73, 74, 76, *77,* 78, 86–92, *90,* 93, 94, 99, 116, 117, 118, 122, 138, 149

Walsh, Ed, 52, 54, 59, 67, 73, 74, 75, 86, 93, 143, 149

Washington Senators, 28, 70, 71, 100, 120, 129

Western League, 20, 21, 22, 23

Young, Denton "Cy," 12, 17, 25, 26, 34, 35, 42, 43, 55, 56–59, 60, 63, 74, 75, 86, 105

DATE DUE

DEC 23 1999			
OCT 0 8 2003			
OCT 1 5 2003			
OCT 0 5 2004			
OCT 1 3			
6			
OCT 3			
SEP 2 8			
MAR 0 1 OCT 0 1 2007			

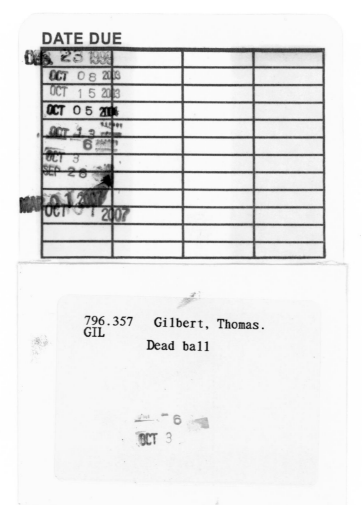

796.357
GIL   Gilbert, Thomas.

        Dead ball

            6

    OCT 3